# About the Author

Paul Roland is a qualified counsellor and teacher of mysticism and Kabbalistic meditation. His own mystic experiences began when he was still a child and led him to study various aspects of the esoteric, including practical magic, yoga, meditation, Buddhism and the Kabbalah, the latter with one of the foremost Masters of our time. He is the author of several books including *Prophecies and Predictions* (De Agnosti), *The Complete Book of Dreams* (Hamlyn) and *Revelations – The Wisdom of the Ages* (Carlton Publishing). As a freelance writer he has been a regular contributor to various national publications in Britain, Europe, the United States and Japan including *The Mail on Sunday, The X-Factor, Sightings, Uri Geller's Paranormal Encounters, Alien Encounters, Sounds, Which CD?* and *Classic CD*. He lives in Kent, England with his wife and two children.

## Piatkus Guides

A PIATKUS GUIDE

# Kabbalah

*Paul Roland*

PIATKUS

Neither the author nor the publisher is responsible for any harm caused to anyone undertaking the exercises and meditations in this book. Anyone who has suffered from a mental or emotional illness should seek medical advice before attempting the exercises.

© 1999 Paul Roland

First published in 1999 by
Judy Piatkus (Publishers) Ltd
5 Windmill Street, London W1P 1HF

The moral rights of the author have been asserted

A catalogue record for this book is available from the British Library

ISBN 0-7499-1957-4

Set in 12.5/14pt Perpetua
Typeset by Action Publishing Technology Limited, Gloucester
Printed & bound in Great Britain by
Mackays of Chatham PLC

# Contents

# Dedication

*This book is dedicated to my mother, with love.*

# Introduction

'She is more precious than pearls; and all the things you value are not equal unto her. Length of days is in her right hand; in her left are riches and honour. Her ways are ways of pleasantness, and all her paths are peace. A tree of life is she to those who lay hold of her; and every one that firmly grasps her will be made happy.' – King Solomon, Book of Proverbs

The mere mention of the Kabbalah, the secret Jewish mystical tradition which forms the basis of practical magic and the Western esoteric tradition, often conjures up visions of fantastic realms and forbidden lore in the popular imagination. But what are these arcane secrets shared by the mystics, magicians and prophets throughout the ages? How might we apply them today in a simple, practical way for the purpose of personal development, psychic awareness and spiritual renewal? And what are the teachings that have attracted modern practitioners as diverse as the notorious magician Aleister Crowley and a growing group of contemporary celebrities including pop priestess Madonna?

Traditional Kabbalists may regret such sensational attention, which is usually accompanied by superficial press coverage, but Kabbalah is a living tradition which must speak to each generation if it is to survive. It was never intended to be a fossilised philosophy.

Unfortunately it is a tradition which continues to be much misunderstood and misinterpreted, partly because of its association with shadowy secret societies such as the Hermetic Order of the Golden Dawn, and partly because its early practitioners deliberately enshrouded its secrets in obscure symbolism for fear of being accused of practising the Black Arts. For 2,000 years its secrets have been guarded for good reason. However, now is not a time for secrets, but for revelations.

## 'As Above, So Below'

One of the most positive human characteristics is our insatiable curiosity, our restless longing to find out what lies beyond our immediate experience. And yet, as our knowledge of the physical universe increases and our technological achievements threaten to overtake our capacity to control them, we appear no nearer to understanding our own nature nor the purpose of our existence. I suspect that even the most materialistic person will admit, if only to themselves, to having at one time experienced a sense of something beyond their comprehension, something outside the confines of the physical world, which could give a meaning and purpose to their life.

Practising Kabbalists, myself included, do not claim an exclusive right or access to the truth. In Kabbalah there is no absolute truth, only the truth of the Absolute. Instead Kabbalah offers a symbolic interpretation of existence and our place and purpose in it, which can be verified to some extent in theory and practice.

Kabbalah is a unified scheme which is deceptively and divinely simple. It demonstrates that what appears to our limited intellects to be confusion, disorder and chaos is in fact ordered, purposeful and evolving exactly as its Creator intended. Most importantly everyone can experience the truth of this system for themselves. Kabbalah is a means by which we can use devotion, contemplation and action to enable us to understand the nature of the Divine through its manifested aspects. The following chapters use practical methods and techniques to experience the Divine forces, energies and qualities as they are manifest in ourselves, the world around us and the invisible realms beyond.

From an early age I had many mystical experiences – including out-of-body experiences and glimpses of past lives – which fascinated and exhilarated me, but I had no means to put them into any kind of context, or to attribute them with any lasting significance, until I discovered Kabbalah. Like many of the mystics, magicians and psychics whom I consulted during my teens and early twenties, I was fascinated by unexplained phenomena. But I was also frustrated by the lack of real knowledge needed to make sense of it all and which would help me to harness and develop my natural but unusual abilities.

I knew I would not find the answers I was seeking in religion although, ironically, Kabbalah is the real heart of the religion into which I was born. Although a traditional Jew, I was raised very liberally in a dwindling community whose esoteric tradition was long forgotten. Its ageing members clung to the archaic rituals out of a sense of duty rather than devotion. Or at least, that is how it seemed to me at the time.

In such circumstances I despaired of finding the teacher that the age-old proverb promised would appear when the pupil is ready. But then a friend introduced me to the Kabbalah, and everything fell into place. It explained the structure of existence, the purpose of creation and spiritual evolution in terms which gave dignity and value to each human life. It also answered how it was possible for suffering to exist in a world created by a loving God. These were not glib, fundamentalist solutions, demanding blind faith from those who subscribed to them. Each could be and were tested again and again. One of the Kabbalah's strengths is that it requires its practitioners to constantly question and test everything they are told to see if it rings 'true' for them.

In time I became a teacher of Kabbalah and meditation myself, and I also wrote several books on esoteric subjects, mysticism and comparative religions. So, for me, Kabbalah is not a fashionable New Age religion. Nor is it an intellectual indulgence reserved exclusively for rabbinical scholars. In fact, few of the people I have taught over the years have been Jewish. No knowledge of Judaism or even of the Hebrew language is necessary, or even desirable. The Kabbalah expresses a universal wisdom, albeit presented in a unique diagrammatic and philosophical form. Furthermore, it does not require strict training, or an ascetic lifestyle. It is a practical system of self-awareness, personal development and spiritual evolution. Its teachings and values have to be tried and tested against the stresses and strains of modern life and in the intense give and take of conventional human relationships, otherwise the highs and the insights gained in meditation are a mere virtual reality rollercoaster ride.

This book aims to demystify what many readers might have assumed is a complex and archaic philosophy shrouded in obscure symbolism, its secrets deciphered exclusively by

the orthodox rabbis from profound and impenetrable philosophical commentaries on the Hebrew sacred texts. By
working with the principles of the Kabbalah its initiates can
experience the higher realms for themselves and gain knowledge from the beings which exist there. One of the main
purposes of this book is to help you tap these same sources of
wisdom and power safely by the more modern but equally
effective methods of pathworking and creative visualisation.
And by so doing prove the value and teachings for yourself.

'On penetrating into the sanctuary of the Kabbalah one is
seized with admiration in the presence of a doctrine so
logical, so simple and at the same time so absolute ... a
philosophy simple as the alphabet, profound and infinte as
the Word; theorems more complete and luminous than
those of Pythagoras ... All truly dogmatic religions have
issued from the Kabbalah and return therein. Whatsoever
is grand or scientific in the religious dreams of the
illuminated, of Jacob Bohme, Swedenborg, Saint-Martin
and the rest, is borrowed from the Kabbalah; all Masonic
Associations owe to it their secrets and their symbols ...
it establishes, by the counterpoise of two forces in apparent opposition, the eternal balance of being...' – Eliphas
Levi, *Transcendental Magic*.

This quote reveals what a learned occultist thought of
Kabbalah and gives an impression of how his fellow mystics
revered the tradition even though their interpretation is a
little fanciful.

In accordance with tradition, whereby all initiates of the
teaching are encouraged to make it clear that their understanding of Kabbalah is a personal one, I am obliged to point
out that what follows is my own interpretation of Kabbalah as

passed down to me by my teachers and filtered through revelation and my personal experiences.

(Note: Kabbalah, Cabbala/Cabala, Qabalah are simply
interchangeable variations – there is no significance behind
one spelling over another.)

# Meditation

The visualisation exercises in this book have been created by
me to help both the newcomer and the experienced meditator to develop greater self-awareness and safely experience
the higher states of consciousness. Anybody who has under-
gone serious mental or emotional problems or has a nervous
disposition should seek professional medical advice before
considering whether to attempt the exercises.

## Helpful Hints For Successful Meditation

The first rule of meditation is to relax. Although this may
appear to be an obvious suggestion, it is nevertheless a fact
that many people who meditate – including some who
consider themselves to be experienced – are so eager to
achieve something in meditation that they don't truly relax.
They have expectations of achieving enlightenment or of
receiving some form of revelationary vision, and consequently they try too hard. Don't try. Still the mind and let
go. Give the sleeping giant within you, your Higher Self, a
chance to awaken. Think of meditation as being similar to
swimming, where the more relaxed you are, and the less
effort you make, the easier you will float, buoyed up by the
water. In both cases, if you tense up and try to impose your
will, you will sink! To use another metaphor, it is like the
child who plants a seed and then stands over it willing it to
grow. When the flower of your own spirit has had sufficient

light and nourishment then be certain that it will blossom.

The second rule of meditation is to be patient. It is like any form of exercise, in that the more you practise the easier it will become and the more potent will be the power that you are eventually able to draw upon.

If you have not meditated before, or are of a nervous nature, remember that you are not going anywhere, so there is no need for fear. You are always in control and can end the exercise at any time. You are expanding your consciousness, your awareness and tapping latent inner resources for your own highest good. Remember the universal law that 'Like attracts like'. No harm or negative influence will come to you if your intentions are good and directed towards your own self-development. However, if you are uncomfortable at any point simply count down from ten to one in your mind. You will probably find the anxiety disappears before you reach five. Then you can rejoin the exercise. After each meditation is is important to ground yourself to regain your balance and sense of reality, for example by drinking a glass of water, washing your face and hands with cold water, taking a refreshing shower or going for a short walk, preferably in a natural environment such as a garden or park.

Finally, I must stress the importance of always testing for deception. Many authors and teachers ignore the importance of this, an omission which I consider to be grossly irresponsible. The mind is like a monkey that does not take to being trained. Even the most dedicated, experienced and spiritually aware person is prey to the mind's restless nature, continual distractions and power to delude and deceive. It is imperative to always test for deception during meditations where contact is being sought with inner or external forces and whenever images come to consciousness that the meditator senses are not products of their own imagination. Such images can be impressions from the astral plane, a more subtle world where our thoughts take form when focused by the will. Alternatively they can be archetypal images, memories or communications from disincarnate beings. To check for deception simply say any sacred name or prayer and the image will break up if the contact is not a true one. For the purposes of this book I will use the traditional Hebrew names which have been tried and tested through the centuries. But if you do not respond to these feel free to substitute whatever feels right for you. If the source is truly Divine, it will not be offended that you simply wish to confirm that this is so.

For practical purposes it is recommended that, to avoid having to continually refer to the text, you record the scripts of the various exercises on to cassette, perhaps with a background of suitably inspiring music or natural sound effects to create a relaxing atmosphere.

## EXERCISE: GROUNDING, CLEARING AND PROTECTING

This exercise should be done at the beginning of each and every meditation session. It not only grounds you so that you are not overwhelmed or unbalanced by excessive energy, but also cleanses your mental, emotional and etheric bodies and protects you from any external influences other than those of a Divine nature.

☆ Sit down and make yourself comfortable with your back straight, feet flat on the floor and slightly apart, and hands on your thighs.

☆ Close your eyes and begin to focus on your breath. Take slow deep regular breaths.

☆ When you exhale, imagine that you are expelling tension in the form of a grey mist. Consider this to be a form of energy pollution which you have involuntarily absorbed with the stress and pressure of modern life. You now realise that you don't need it. It is inhibiting, clouding the real radiant being that you know yourself to be. Expel the tension with every exhalation.

☆ When you inhale, breathe in a golden light which glows like the mellow sunlight on a still summer evening. It warms and calms you with every breath. Exhale the tension and all the foreign dross that had settled on you like city smog, and inhale a calm, fresh summer evening glow. Feel yourself relaxing with every breath.

☆ Now focus on a point just above your head. Imagine a sphere of radiant, shimmering incandescent light hovering over you like a small sun. It is a source of Divine power complementing that which burns within you eternally. The sphere contains the revitalising energy that you need at this moment and which is yours by right. You are a Divine being. As such you can call upon this source of love and light at any time.

☆ Now allow the sphere to be absorbed through the crown of your head. Sense its light and energy moving down through your head, relaxing your scalp, forehead, face and jaw. Imagine it dissolving the tension as it runs like a warm refreshing shower down your neck, your chest and back, along your arms and legs and out through your fingers and toes.

☆ Feel the warmth of the light now pulsing within you. Sense its radiant glow moving down through your chest, stomach and solar plexus, the seat of the emotions. Become aware of any blocks in these places. Imagine them cracking and coming apart like a block of concrete under pressure. See the pieces being ground into smaller and smaller fragments until they are merely dust to be dispersed into the aura and blown away into the outside world. Focus your attention on your back, hips and legs and feel the light coursing like a shower of golden light as it washes away the last drops of tension through your toes.

☆ As it runs out, imagine you are sending fibrous roots of etheric energy down into the earth. Feel them going deep into the soil, gaining a firm grip. This will ground you and also give you an outlet to channel any excess energy which you may feel unable to handle at the present moment. It will serve you just like a lightning conductor.

☆ Now imagine a second sphere emerging from the earth, rising until it is under your feet. Begin to draw its healing light up through those roots and into your body, through your feet, legs, back, solar plexus and stomach. Draw it up through your fingertips, into your hands, arms, chest, neck and head. Let it merge and blend with the energising light still pouring down from the crown.

☆ Now you are a clear and open channel of celestial and terrestrial energy. From head to toe you are luminous with the light that has permeated every cell of your being and at every level – in the physical, mental and emotional bodies.

☆ You are cleansed, energised and grounded. Even if you are not consciously aware of it, you will be protected in this cloak of light of your own making for the remainder of the day. Bask in the light as if you were spiritually sunbathing for a few minutes. Now become aware of your breathing once again and of your body, the chair you are sitting in, your surroundings.

☆ When you are ready, open your eyes.

# 1

# The Golden Thread

## Guarding the Secrets

'Rabbi Simeon sat and wept, and he said, "Woe if I reveal these secrets and woe if I do not reveal them." The companions (initiates) who were there remained silent until Rabbi Abba stood and said to him, "If our master wishes to reveal these matters, is it not written, 'The secret of the Lord belongs to those who fear Him' and do not those companions tremble before the Holy One, blessed be He?"'

These lines from the *Sefer ha Zohar* (*The Book of Splendour*), a Jewish mystical text from the 13th century, suggest that the body of profound secret teachings known as Kabbalah, which forms the foundation of the Western esoteric tradition, was to be regarded as the exclusive preserve of Jewish mystics.

That was certainly the belief of initiates who, from Biblical times to the latter years of the 20th century, considered themselves to have been chosen by God to guard the secrets of life and death from the eyes of the profane. In fact, so fearful were the early Jewish mystics of betraying God's trust that they encoded their secrets in the allegorical fables and teachings of the Torah. The Torah translates as 'The Teaching/Instruction' meaning both oral and written teaching. When it is written as *Sefer ha Torah* (*The Book of Instruction*) it refers to the written part only which is the Pentateuch (the five books of Moses in the Old Testament). It was then left for the more enlightened rabbis to transmit the hidden meaning orally to their pupils, a practice which gave the teaching its name, for Kabbalah means 'receiving'. More conservative rabbis and scholars of the Orthodox tradition considered only the outer teaching, the letter of the law rather than the spirit of the Torah, and condemned the Kabbalists as heretics. Their attitude persists to this day.

Through the centuries a small number of initiates inevitably confided their knowledge to non-Jews, who in turn considered themselves to be custodians of the Hokhmah Nistarah, the Hidden Wisdom. Some were learned men of science and the occult such as Agrippa von Nettesheim (1486–1535) and the scholar magician Paracelsus (?1493–1541) the precursor of homeopathy, who used their knowledge and understanding of the universal laws to lay the foundations for modern chemistry, physics and medicine. (The universal laws are the natural laws operating equally in all dimensions – which are of course not limited to the Kabbalistic teachings. For example, 'Like attracts like' meaning that all those who act in accordance with the Divine will for the highest good of all humanity will receive assistance from both their inner teacher and benign external forces. Another example would be that negative actions and thoughts always rebound to affect the person who is creating them.)

Secret societies formed at various moments in history

which perpetuated and practised the arcane secrets which had been culled from various traditions – such as the Freemasons and the Hermetic Order of the Golden Dawn. These groups took the teachings underground, incorporating them into their doctrines and rituals. But the founders of these brotherhoods (which were initially exclusively for men) also had a keen interest in and knowledge of other mystery traditions (the esoteric teachings of the ancients), such as the Egyptian magical rituals, the Christian Grail legends, the Rosicrucian myths and the Greek mysteries. From these they incorporated elements which they thought were appropriate or, in some instances, merely exotic.

Perhaps because of this dilution of the original teachings beyond Judaism, and as a result of the deliberate obscuring of the simple truths behind the Biblical fables by some of the Jews themselves in an effort to preserve their secrets, the image of Kabbalah as a complex and impenetrable system has stubbornly persisted. Certainly, it continues to be much misunderstood and misinterpreted by both Jews and non-Jews alike.

## Origins

Many myths surround the Kabbalah and veil its true origins. Its secrets are supposed to have been entrusted to Adam in the Garden of Eden by the archangel Raziel so that humankind could regain entry to Paradise. All that can be said with certainty is that the earliest written teachings are preserved in the Torah, or Book of Instruction, which was rediscovered by Josiah, King of Judah, in Solomon's Temple in 700 BCE. The Torah takes the form of an allegorical history of the Hebrew people that can be considered to be the sum of the spiritual insights revealed to the Hebrew prophets and patriarchs, beginning with the mythic figure of Abraham, 'father of the Hebrew people'.

During the Second Temple period of Jewish history (6th century BCE–1st century CE) what we now know as the Kabbalah was developing into a practical spiritual discipline under the name Maaseh Merkabah (Work of the Chariot), a title derived from Ezekiel's vision of a celestial chariot. Ezekiel, the Hebrew prophet of the 6th century BCE, was the author of visionary texts which have profoundly influenced Jewish mystical thought and practice. Outside of the tradition the vision in which the prophet described a fiery chariot drawn by four winged creatures each with four faces is commonly interpreted as symbolic of the apocalypse to come at the end of the world. In contrast, the Kabbalist understands that the vision was a revelation of a greater reality, the structure of existence, and not a prediction.

## Secret Sects

In Biblical times such knowledge as the true meaning of Ezekiel's vision was deemed to be the exclusive preserve of the Hebrew mystics and the initiates of the various ascetic mystical sects that flourished throughout Palestine. The most historically significant of these were the Essenes, who established what was probably the first Kabbalistic monastery at Qumran in what is now Jordan around 200 BCE in an effort to isolate themselves from the orthodox Hebrew priests whom they considered to be corrupt. (A neighbouring group were the Nazarenes, of whom Joshua ben Miriam, more commonly known as Jesus, is believed to have been an initiate.) It is possible that the Essenes were the descendants of the elect to whom Moses had imparted the esoteric (hidden) teachings that he received on Mount Sinai, while the mass of the Israelites were taught only the exoteric (outer) doctrine in the form of the Ten Commandments in order to keep the faith.

Moses received the complete Torah (the teaching) on Mount Sinai, which was later divided into the written and oral teachings. The former formed the basis of the Bible and the latter formed the laws, stories, religious practices and esoteric wisdom preserved in the Talmud. Unfortunately confusion arises from the fact that the so-called oral tradition is preserved in written form in the Talmud, but consider this similar to a written record of a discussion and all might be clearer. Significantly, the sacred texts of the Essenes, which have recently been translated from a number of sources including the Dead Sea Scrolls, differ from the Old Testament versions in encouraging initiates to honour their Heavenly Father and their Earthly Mother rather than their parents, a concept of cosmic duality which is alien to Orthodox Judaism.

From what we know of the Essenes they appear to have practised a variation on Maaseh Merkabah (Work of the Chariot, which was the study of man) and Maaseh Berashit (Work of Creation, which was the study of the universe), which later developed into classical Kabbalah. This involved a form of yoga in which they sought to harmonise the complementary attributes of the Earthly Mother and Heavenly Father within the subtle energy centres of their own body, at points roughly corresponding to the chakras of Eastern philosophy.

The sect identified the existence of seven terrestrial 'angels' of the Earthly Mother (sun, water, air, earth, life, joy and the Earthly Mother herself) and seven celestial 'angels' of the Heavenly Father (power, love, wisdom, eternal life, creative work, peace and the Eternal Father) with whom they communed each morning and evening. These aspects correspond closely with the Divine attributes of the Kabbalistic system.

To assist with their meditations on the qualities and purpose of each 'angel', the Essenes contemplated a symbol which they called the Tree of Life which may have been the earliest version of the central Kabbalistic glyph which also bears that name. This idea was subsequently refined to become the diagram we know today. The Essene tree has much in common with the sacred Bodhai tree of Buddhism, the World Tree of shamanism and Yggdrasil, the World Tree of Nordic mythology, in that it depicts seven branches stretching heavenwards and seven roots penetrating the earth, with Man as the trunk balancing the forces of the upper and lower levels of manifestation.

## Sacred Books

A key development in the evolution of classical Kabbalah was the discovery of the *Sefer ha Yetzirah* (*The Book of Creation*) in the 3rd century CE. The earliest references to this appear in texts of the 1st century CE. This anonymous work, attributed to Abraham, the Father of the Hebrew people, is essentially a meditative manual with distinct magical overtones. Whatever the identity of the anonymous author, he had evidently gathered disparate strands of the teaching from the communities in Babylon and Palestine and had woven them into a seamless whole. Much of Kabbalistic cosmology is derived from the Babylonian influence (the wisdom of the ancient kingdom of Mesopotamia c.3000 BCE), which envisages a universe inhabited by a hierarchy of angels and demons, while the Jewish mystical tradition of Palestine, with its strong Platonic influence (from the teachings of the ancient Greek philosopher, Plato (?427–?347 BCE), provides the foundation of its philosophy.

With reference to these divergent traditions, the *Sefer ha Yetzirah* set down the principles of the sephirotic system for the first time – the ten Divine attributes were described as ten spheres, each linked by a network of paths corresponding to the 22 letters of the Hebrew alphabet.

From this point on, numbers and letters were considered to have supernatural significance for both mystics and magicians. The 13th-century Kabbalist Abraham Abulafia believed that decoding the occult significance of numbers and letters would reveal the key to the mysteries and that whoever deciphered these secrets would have no need to await the Messiah because he would become his own saviour. 'Everyone knows that the letters of our alphabet can be classified as individuals, species and genera,' he wrote. 'Every letter is affected by accidents arising from either matter or form.'

A second theme of the *Sefer ha Yetzirah* is that words themselves hold power and for that reason the spoken word is held to be a medium for the act of creation. It is a belief embodied in one sentence: 'Every creature and every word comes from a single name.' The name referred to is the secret name of God, the same name which the Gospel of St John refers to: 'In the beginning was the word and the word was with God and the word was God.'

Unfortunately, anti-Semitic elements frequently mistook this metaphysical theory, either maliciously or out of simple ignorance, as proof that Jews were practitioners of the Black Arts. They voiced the suspicion that the *Sefer ha Yetzirah* included a formula for empowering a clay figure with artificial life, a concept which gave rise to the legend of the Golem (from the Hebrew word for 'formless thing'). The legend (of unknown origin and date) and the practice of creating a thought form became confused so that we cannot know if the legend grew from exaggerated reports of the meditative practice or if the practice was inspired by the principle of man's ability to create life in his own image as God had done. But this took too literally what is in practice an advanced meditative exercise, for the Kabbalist does not make a physical figure, but attempts to focus his own creative powers to project a thought form into the astral realm in the image of a man. Such activity has been a standard spiritual discipline in many traditions for thousands of years, most notably in Tibet, where these projections of the imagination are known as Tulpa creations. The practice is continued (albeit unconsciously) in modern spiritual healing, where the healer's energies are often channelled into an angelic or amorphous thought form, such as a ball of light, before being sent out to revitalise the absent patient.

Until the 19th century such concepts were well beyond the understanding of a superstitious public who largely continued to regard the Jews with suspicion. Consequently, practitioners couched their secrets in ever more obscure symbolism for fear of giving their persecutors another excuse for a pogrom. In the 16th century, Isaac Lura wrote: 'For every hand's breadth [of the mysteries] I reveal, I will hide a mile. With great difficulty I will open the gates of holiness, making an opening like the eye of a needle, and let him who is worthy pass through it to enter the innermost chamber.'

## The Tradition in Europe

From Babylon the hidden wisdom was communicated to Europe in the 9th century by Aaron ben Samuel, a Jewish Kabbalist. The more practical and occult form took root in

Germany in the Middle Ages, where Kabbalah was stripped of its commentaries on the possible meanings of the Talmud and so forth, and its principles were used to practise ritual magic instead. The philosophical or theoretical form was developed elsewhere in Europe. In medieval Italy, France and Flanders the more speculative aspects were seized upon by scholars eager to reinterpret the philosophy of Kabbalah in the then fashionable language of Neoplatonism, which stated that all things emanated from a single transcendent Godhead. This atmosphere of intense learned debate and re-evaluation allowed the ancient teachings to take a form that modern practitioners would recognise as classical Kabbalah with its triple approach to enlightenment or unification – that of action, contemplation and devotion.

The teaching of Kabbalah extended across eastern Europe before stretching out to root in northern Africa, the Turkish Empire and the Orient with the migrating Hasidic Jews of Eastern Europe and the Sephardic Jews exiled from Portugal and Spain at the end of the 15th century. By the 18th century the tradition had found fertile roots in America where it came to enjoy a significant revival in the late 20th century.

## The Book of Splendour

The *Sefer ha Zohar* (*The Book of Splendour*), whose circulation in 13th-century Spain instigated the golden age of Kabbalistic scholarship in Europe, is considered to be the second most significant text in classical Kabbalah. Together with the *Sefer ha Yetzirah* and the *Sefer ha Torah* it forms the cornerstone of Kabbalistic literature.

Even in modern translation its language appears as deliberately obscure as the teachings of the Torah that it is attempting to clarify. Compiled by Rabbi Moses ben

Shemtov of Léon from many anonymous sources, its commentaries on the secret meanings of the Torah continue to absorb and confound scholars to the present day. 'Ignorant people consider only the clothes that are the story; they see nothing more than that and do not realise what the clothes conceal. Those who know a little better see not only the clothes but the body beneath them. The wise ... consider only the soul, which is the essence of the real Torah.' – *Sefer ha Zohar*.

In each generation the Kabbalist is expected to reinterpret the sacred texts in the light of their own understanding and argue in favour of these with their teacher rather than merely subscribe to accepted dogma. This is what makes it a living tradition, one which, for example, can today be transmitted in terms of modern psychology.

As was the custom in the Middle Ages, Rabbi Shemtov attributed the book to a legendary figure, Rabbi Yokhai, in order to lend the work greater authority, so Rabbi Yokhai's discussion of the mysteries of existence with his followers forms the greater part of the text. Their exchanges reveal the origins of the universe and its eternal laws, as well as the forms in which they manifest in man.

At one point Rabbi Yokhai is asked why man has an incarnation on earth if he also has the certain knowledge that he must endure suffering and one day die. The answer which Rabbi Yokhai gives reveals the central secret of the Torah and a recurrent theme of the Kabbalah: human beings are incarnations of the immortal Divine spark, seeking to know the nature of God through experience, knowledge and understanding of his creation. Only through direct involvement in this 'rite of passage' that we call life can we affect the course of creation.

# Christian Kabbalists

Giovanni Pico della Mirandola and Johann Reuchlin were leading Christian scholars of the Renaissance. In the 15th century, attempting to purge the Kabbalah of its 'pagan' elements, they stripped the tradition of its spiritual significance, leaving only the bare structure of the sephirotic Tree of Life, festooned with unintelligible letters and names to enchant and bemuse the philosophers, magicians and theologians of subsequent centuries.

Mirandola (1463–94 CE), who had acquired his knowledge of Kabbalah from a converted Jew, was convinced that the Jewish mystical system was the golden thread connecting the ancient Greek philosophy of Plato and Pythagoras with Christianity. In deciphering some of its more obscure commentaries, he thought he had found an explanation for the incarnation of Christ as being the living manifestation of the Word of God. After publishing his conclusions in 1486 under the title *Conclusiones Philosophicae, Cabalisticae Et Theologicae* he was condemned by the church as a heretic for promoting what the authorities considered to be the practice of magic and for insisting that 'angels only understand Hebrew'! Mirandola, however, remained unrepentant, retorting: 'Magic is the highest and holiest form of philosophy.'

Johann Reuchlin (1455–1522 CE), a former German embassy attaché, was more diplomatic in his attempts to convince the church to adopt the principles of the Kabbalah, although ultimately he was no more successful than his predecessor. While researching his seminal work *De Arte Cabalistica* (known as *The Bible of the Christian Cabala*), Reuchlin was fortunate to be able to refer to a number of authentic Hebrew manuscripts, given to him by the grateful rabbis of Pforzheim, on whose behalf he had interceded after

Emperor Maximilian I had condemned all Hebrew books to be burned.

An intense study of the Pforzheim manuscripts led Reuchlin to the belief that God 'revealed His secrets to man in Hebrew' and that these secrets are encoded in the Kabbalah, which he described as 'a symbolic theology, in which letters and names are not only the signs for things, but also their very essence'. Decoding the secrets led him to declare that he had discovered 'the correct spelling of the name of Jesus' and the 'ultimate meaning' of His coming. But even after dedicating his book to Pope Leo X in the hope of avoiding the unwelcome attentions of the Inquisition, Reuchlin also failed to convince the Church authorities to look favourably upon what he ardently believed to be an expression of the shared universal truth at the heart of all the world's religions.

These earnest and learned men were determined to appropriate the Kabbalah for the Church. To do so they went to extraordinary lengths to prove that the configuration of the sephiroth and the sacred texts of the Hebrews had predicted the coming of Christ. By selectively manipulating numbers and letters they managed to convince themselves that the Old Testament was fundamentally Christian in character and that Christianity was the natural successor to Judaism.

However, it is self-evident that the Christian concept of original sin, in which Man is estranged from God through sin, is incompatible with the Kabbalistic belief that Man is only separated from the Divine source through his own ignorance. Furthermore, as Kabbalah requires every initiate to test the truth of the teachings for themselves, it cannot subscribe to the idea that a priest, or even a rabbi, can set themselves up as a mediator between a man and his God. Moreover, ortho-dox Christianity adheres to the belief that faith, good deeds and strict observance of doctrine are the fundamental requirements for eternal life. In contrast, the Kabbalist understands that self-knowledge is the only sure way to salvation, or more accurately, to fulfil the will of God.

## Freemasonry

It is not known precisely how or when Kabbalistic concepts became an integral element of Masonic ritual, but it appears that its symbols are literally woven into the fabric of this philanthropic secret society. The order was founded in London in 1717, but its origins go back to the medieval guilds of itinerant stone masons.

Every Masonic temple is designed along Kabbalistic principles, with the two pillars of Divine duality fronting the entrance door and featuring as a focal point in the main hall in remembrance of Solomon's Temple. The floor of the central chamber in which the Masonic rituals take place has a chequered design, symbolising the interdependence of universal forces. These symbols are repeated in the main teaching aid known as the tracing board, an illustrated board which also depicts the sun and the moon in the sky above the temple, illustrating the idea that the same principles which govern the earth also operate in the heavens. Between these is often found the Most Holy name of God, the Great Architect of the Universe, inscribed in Hebrew. Below this, linking heaven and earth, is Jacob's Ladder, whose three rungs represent the three higher worlds (Emanation, Creation and Formation, see pages 43–7). Masonic terminology renames them faith, hope and charity to reflect the attributes required of the members at each level or degree of initiation.

In its rituals too, the Masons preserve the secret doctrine

which is unique to the Kabbalah. In the ritual of the Second Degree, for example, the initiate is informed of the Kabbalistic concept of creation, albeit in technical terminology. He is told of the 'regular progression of science from a point to a line, from a line to a plane, from a plane to a solid'. This analogy makes him aware that every aspect of creation is an extension of its source and carries the essence of the three stages through which it has passed in its descent from the celestial to the terrestrial world.

Leo Tolstoy referred to these Kabbalistic principles in his novel *War and Peace* using the voice of an anonymous character who professed to be a member of the Masons: 'The first and chief object of our Order, the foundation on which it rests and which no human power can destroy, is the preservation and handing on to posterity of a certain important mystery, which has come down to us from the remotest ages, even from the first man – a mystery on which perhaps the fate of mankind depends. But since this mystery is of such a nature that nobody can know or use it unless he be prepared by long and diligent self-purification, not everyone can hope to attain it quickly. Hence we have a secondary aim: that of preparing our members as much as possible to reform their hearts, to purify and enlighten their minds, by means handed on to us by tradition.'

The Masonic guilds of the Middle Ages sought to preserve these same secrets in the structure of Europe's great cathedrals, which were modelled on the Temple of Solomon, itself a symbol of the Four Worlds of existence.

## The Golden Dawn

By the 19th century the ageless wisdom of Kabbalah had became so obscured by the efforts of those determined to prove that it was all things to all men that Orthodox Judaism had condemned the practice of Kabbalah as contrary to the scriptures. The tradition was further tainted by its association with the more dubious aspects of occultism. The Tree of Life and its teachings were appropriated by those dabbling in ritual magic for secular rather than spiritual ends. Extravagant claims by pompous, self-appointed 'authorities' such as Eliphas Levi and A. E. Waite, who speculated about the Kabbalah's Egyptian origins and its application in divination and the invocation of spirits, only served to strengthen the resolve of the genuine practitioners to keep their secrets to themselves.

The Hermetic Order of the Golden Dawn was an occult secret society which flourished in Victorian England in the wake of a wave of interest in spiritualism, but it attempted to set itself apart from the murky world of mediums and psychic phenomena. Instead it promoted the Order as the custodian of the archaic wisdom and magical practices of the ancient world. Its members included such diverse individuals as the poet W. B. Yeats, the eccentric occultist S. L. MacGregor Mathers (author of *The Kabbalah Unveiled*) and the notorious magician Aleisteir Crowley. It is still a matter of debate whether they are to be praised for disseminating its secrets, or damned for doing so in such a way as to make them appear even more mystifying.

The Order utilised the stages of Divine descent as symbolised by the spheres on the Tree of Life to denote the ten grades of its own hierarchy. A new initiate would therefore be assigned the title of Zelator, equating with the lowest point on the Tree, Malkhut (the Kingdom or earth), rising to a fully realised master, Ipsissimus, which equated with Keter (the Crown or spirit). The five so-called 'Knowledge Lectures' which served as the foundation of the Order's

magical rites included a discourse on the symbolic significance of the Hebrew alphabet as it relates to the sephiroth,
the use of the Divine and archangelic names in invocation and
explanations of how to work with the forces of the Tree of
Life in meditations, rites and rituals.

It also incorporated elements of Egyptian and Enochian
magic into a framework of Rosicrucian ritual to accommodate members from Christian and Masonic backgrounds.
Egyptian magic focused on assuming a god-form, which
involved manifesting the characteristics of a specific god
within the practitioner's personality, and Enochian magic
was a form of spurious angelic magic derived from invoca-
tions which are alleged to have been channelled by an
Elizabethan psychic called Edmund Kelley.

In retrospect the Golden Dawn's eclectic teachings and
theatrical rituals made for an impressive but ultimately spurious synthesis of occult theory and practice, drawing
principally on the magical tradition of mediaeval Europe,
which was essentially Kabbalistic.

## Modern Kabbalah

One of the unique aspects of Kabbalah is that it is a living
tradition. It is – and always has been – adaptable to the needs
and circumstances of successive generations. While in the
past it has proven both a rich source of mystical lore and a
firm foundation for a system of practical magic, it is now
being reinterpreted by modern masters as a means of self-
analysis and self-development.

Contemporary Kabbalists highlight the tradition's potential for personal development, concentrating on the ever
reverberating parallels between the physical, the psyche and
the spirit. Such teachings lie at the heart of the true tradition,

depicting the perfect balance between the psychic, psychological and spiritual aspects. The magical elements are transformed into an enlightening inner exploration rather than externalised in elaborate ceremonial rites and rituals.

Elements of the tradition have been adopted to supplement areas as diverse as dreamwork, psychotherapy, and women's spirituality. In these fields its tone is less scholarly and more user-friendly. It stresses the New Age aspect now being imposed on the age-old teachings, though in purging the tradition of both its occult and Jewish aspects there is a danger of Kabbalah becoming little more than another alternative philosophy.

For 2,000 years the secrets of the Kabbalah have been guarded for good reason. Now it is for each generation to undertake their own rite of passage in search of spiritual development and self-discovery, just as children must experience the world for themselves, regardless of how accurately their parents have described both its joys and its dangers.

# 2

# Basic Principles: The Tree of Life

'Ten Sefiroth out of Nothing. Ten not nine. Ten not eleven. Understand this is Wisdom and in Wisdom understand. Enquire and ponder through their meaning so as to return the Creator to His Throne.' — *Sefer ha Yetzirah*

## In the Beginning

According to Kabbalistic tradition, in the beginning God the Immanent, the Absolute All (AYIN SOF), emerged from God the Transcendent, the Absolute Nothing (AYIN). What was once pure consciousness had condensed into a composite entity.

It is said that the universe came into being because God wished to behold and know Itself. To do so It contracted to leave a void in which It could manifest through realms of increasing density from pure energy to solid matter, in a process not unlike that which occurs when steam condenses into water and finally solidifies as ice. We should therefore consider every atom in the universe as an expression of the Divine.

It seems incomprehensible that something which was and is perfect should seek to manifest itself in existence. But what is perfect does not necessarily evolve. Kabbalah teaches that God cannot truly know Itself unless It sends particles of Its own being, in the form of individual souls, to experience the worlds It has created. Our urge to create, a form of individual expression, may be a reflection of that Divine impulse.

In the process of creation the endless light of the Divine will (AYIN SOF AUR), sometimes symbolised as a lightning bolt, was refracted as through a prism at ten different levels before densifying and grounding itself in form and matter.

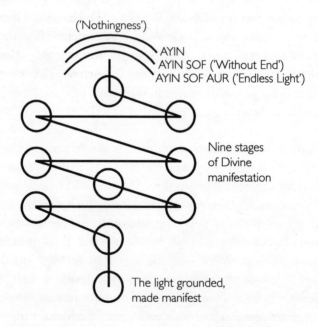

('Nothingness')

AYIN
AYIN SOF ('Without End')
AYIN SOF AUR ('Endless Light')

Nine stages
of Divine
manifestation

The light grounded,
made manifest

The manifestation of the endless light of the Divine will

Each level, known as a sephirah, symbolises the active male and passive female attributes of the Creator and all that It created. Such symbols are grossly inadequate in explaining the nature of the Creator and the immensity of Its creation for these are abstract concepts beyond human comprehension. But Kabbalah offers an intelligible and unified system whereby we can experience the various complementary Divine attributes as they manifest in man, who is created in the image of the Divine.

## Divine Attributes

The sephiroth may be considered as personifying the characteristics of the Supreme Being (Keter), a Heavenly Mother/Father figure, who possesses Wisdom (Hokhmah), Understanding (Binah), Mercy (Hesed), Judgement (Gevurah), Beauty (Tiferet), Love (Nezah), All-Knowledge (Hod), Strength and Perception (Yesod) and Experience (Malkhut).

Human beings were created in the image of the Divine and so possess these same complementary qualities within them. However, having been separated from the source, we are constantly at the mercy of our mutable emotions, our distorted sense of reality and the conflict between spiritual growth and physical indulgence.

You will note that these attributes differ slightly from those indicated on the diagram of the Tree (see page 33). Hebrew words have several meanings, and the traditional Hebrew names used here do not have a direct equivalent in modern English. It is necessary to understand that the Hebrew names are themselves approximate terms for qualities whose essence is beyond our understanding or experience. The traditional translations are given on the diagram, but I have attempted to personalise them in the text to show their adaptability according to the context in which they appear. While we are incarnate we are in a similar situation to our prehistoric ancestors, whose understanding of the universe was limited to whatever they could see between their own cave and the horizon. Each practising Kabbalist must interpret these general terms for themselves through reconciling personal insight with tradition.

## *The Tree of Life*

Many traditions and belief systems through the centuries have shared the Kabbalistic concept of creation in principle, though their interpretation and symbolism have created variations on the same theme and so differ in detail. What makes Kabbalah unique is that it envisages the descent of the Divine in terms of interlinking and interdependent stages of consciousness which we can all explore and experience for ourselves through action, contemplation and devotion.

To enable the initiate to comprehend these abstract concepts and explore the inner and upper worlds of the spirit, the anonymous authors of the *Sefer ha Zohar* devised a simple symbolic glyph known as the Tree of Life upon which are arranged ten spheres representing the sephiroth interconnected by a series of paths.

Each sphere corresponds to a Divine attribute in descending order of emanation, so that the Tree can be seen as illustrating the DNA-like structure or pattern of all that emanated from the Godhead, both in the microcosmos (man) and the macrocosmos (the universe). The sephiroth are invariably shown arranged upon three pillars (the Pillar of Equilibrium, the Pillar of Severity and the Pillar of Mercy), which symbolise the unmanifest Divine principles that govern them. There are several names for the pillars

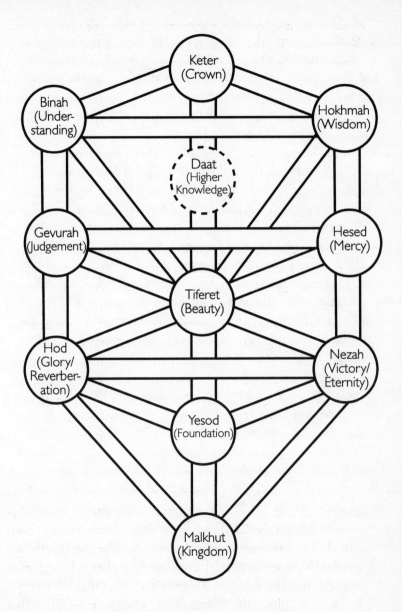

The ten sephiroth within the Tree of Life

depending on context. The names alter to indicate the different tasks at each level. If you are finding these terms too abstract, consider the outer pillars as the forces of expansion and contraction, with Mercy corresponding to the former and Severity to the latter. Under the influence of these two forces the universe continues to expand and evolve under its own momentum.

The male aspects of active force are represented by the three sephiroth on the right-hand Pillar of Mercy while the female aspects of passive form are represented by the three sephiroth on the left-hand Pillar of Severity. The remainder are arranged on the central Pillar of Equilibrium which symbolises the balancing of these complementary qualities.

Keter (the Crown) is the highest point on the Tree. In cosmic terms it can be envisaged as the Godhead, the point of emanation, and in the individual it corresponds to the level of pure consciousness. It is traditionally expressed in the Divine name 'I Am That I Am', which echoes the idea that man is a reflection of his creator.

Coming down the Tree, Hokhmah (Wisdom) is balanced by Binah (Understanding) which together with Keter form the first triad of the Tree at the level of Azilut (Emanation). This is the realm of the Divine will.

From this emanates Gevurah (Judgement) and its complementary attribute Hesed (Mercy). The latter pair form the second triad with Tiferet (Beauty) at the level of Beriah (Creation), where the Divine will to create was defined, but before the universe and its inhabitants were formed.

The three lower sephiroth – Nezah (Eternity), Hod (Reverberation) and Yesod (Foundation) – form the third triad at the level of Yezirah (Formation), which is the realm of archetypes where the model for each species took form prior to materialisation in the physical world. It is the realm mythologised in the Bible as the Garden of Eden.

This Kabbalistic concept echoes the central theme of Plato's philosophy, namely that all life forms and objects in the physical world are expressions of a universal idea beyond the perception of the senses. In effect, there must first exist the idea of an animal, for example, before that animal can manifest in existence. Consequently, if we manipulate the development of certain plants or animals genetically or through selective breeding we are only modifying the form. The blueprint for that species remains in the ether as an ideal model beyond our influence.

The tenth sephirah in order of descent is Malkhut (the Kingdom), which corresponds to the physical world. Although ten spheres are visualised on the Tree, another – Daat (Higher Knowledge) – is shown on the middle pillar between Keter and Tiferet as a broken circle to indicate that it is the unmanifest gateway to the realm of the Divine.

This structure of perpetually unfolding existence is better understood when it is likened to our own creative processes. In the first stage we have an idea that requires the will to see it through. We then draw up plans or blueprints to define the form, decide upon the materials we need and the processes involved before creating the thing itself in physical reality. Each realm that the Creator caused to come into being and everything that evolved and continues to evolve in the momentum of that ongoing process embodies the essence of all that went before it. What has been created is therefore indivisible from the Creator. The sense of separation is an illusion. The practice of a spiritual discipline such as Kabbalah can help to reveal that this is obscuring our vision of the greater reality.

Nothing in the universe exists in isolation. Everything, manifest and unmanifest, affects everything else just as, for example, the smallest muscle movement in our bodies is the final act in a complex chain which begins with the thought of motion and ends with the manipulation of matter.

## The Importance of Balance

To appreciate the practical interplay of the attributes we can consider the example of Joshua ben Miriam, more commonly known as Jesus of Nazareth. As an initiate of the Nazarene sect and a practising Kabbalist, Jesus was able to raise his consciousness to the Yeziratic level, where he could invoke the energies of the third triad. Touching and energising the sephiroth of Nezah, Hod and Tiferet which at the level of the human psyche equate with Unconditional Love, Knowledge (and with it Strength of Character), and the Higher Self (or Inner Teacher) he was able to draw down, or channel, the Christ energy, to overcome the physical forces and perform what the uninitiated considered to be miracles. The Christ energy is a level of heightened awareness and self-realisation corresponding to Tiferet and to the level attained by Jesus – the place of the Inner Teacher or Higher Self also known by Christian Kabbalists as the place of the Cosmic Christ. The apparent contradictions in the gospel accounts, which alternately describe him as being both a radical activist and a gentle pacifist, partly result from the failure of traditional Christian scholars to appreciate that these attributes are not mutually exclusive. Moreover, at the elevated state of consciousness attained by Jesus and other spiritual leaders it is even more critical to maintain the balance.

The key theme in Kabbalah is 'balance'. Having descended from paradise into physical form we become susceptible to the stress and strains of the material world and the influence of its other inhabitants. The attributes that were held in perfect alignment in the higher realms are here subject to distortion and imbalance as one aspect is developed in preference to another.

When the Divine attributes symbolised by the sephiroth are out of balance in the individual it can express itself in ill health (a manifestation of 'dis-ease') or in mental or physical problems. But often the imbalance is more subtle and so less likely to be appreciated by the person who most needs to be aware of it. For example, someone might soak up knowledge like a sponge, but not fully understand or appreciate what they have learned, for knowledge is of little value in itself unless it is balanced by wisdom and understanding. While this may not be critical in the average person, it can have serious repercussions for a scientist, for example, who might be so absorbed in what they are developing that they are unaware of the consequences.

Likewise, someone who does not channel the urge for physical action into a constructive form is likely to seek an outlet for their excess energy in a reckless and potentially hazardous activity such as a dangerous sport or even a criminal activity in which they can satisfy their impulse for excitement.

To take it a stage further, any group of individuals – whether a loose collective of friends, a formal organisation, a localised community or a nation – will unconsciously project their strengths and failings into the larger entity they have created in their own image. Whoever assumes the role of the mother or father (at the level of Keter, the Crown) is then able to exploit an imbalance in the community as a whole and galvanise the entire group into acts of aggression against 'undesirable elements' within or against its neighbours. Often what we perceive as evil is the result of a pathological imbalance and not the influence of a malevolent external force.

Rarely have national leaders and heads of state been able to awaken what can be considered as the passive female qualities, symbolised by the sephiroth on the Pillar of Mercy. Mahatma Gandhi achieved it with his revolution of passive resistance in India, until disruptive elements invoked the more volatile centres of the nation's aggressive male force. More recently, the death of Diana, Princess of Wales touched passive female qualities in the British population, many of whom were confounded by these long neglected feelings. When these sephiroth are temporarily and suddenly awoken without a counterbalance to keep these new-found qualities in proportion it can be quite a shock to the system. No wonder that a few months after her death there was a backlash to what many saw as an unhealthy sentimentalism, for this is a side of the Tree that male-dominated nations prefer to leave in the shade.

The Kabbalah conveys a sense of the completeness and unity of all creation. The universe is a reflection of God. All those who wish to know the nature of their Creator need first to know themselves, for all that is below is a reflection of all that is above.

## EXERCISE: THE HIERARCHY OF CREATION

The following meditation can be done sitting in a chair or lying on a mat on the floor. It is a guided visualisation designed to help you to appreciate and experience the structure of creation and your place in it.

☆ Make yourself comfortable with your back straight. If you are sitting down, place your feet flat on the floor and slightly apart, with your hands on your thighs.

☆ Close your eyes and begin by focusing on your breath. Take slow deep regular breaths. Imagine that you are breathing out tension with every exhalation and breathing in a warm, calming light with every inhalation.

☆ Now visualise yourself standing before the entrance to a cave in a mountainside. You approach the cavernous entrance with pleasant anticipation. Once inside you see that it is illuminated with the reflected light of innumerable crystals. This is the entrance to a world within a world. You descend into the half-light, down endless flights of steps carved into the mountain, passing the multi-coloured layers of rock and the fossilised remains of billions of creatures preserved from the earliest days of the earth's existence.

☆ Very soon you find yourself on a ledge overlooking a cauldron of molten rock at the very centre of the earth, where the prima mater, the basic elements of life, bubble in their raw state. The heat is intense but you are unaffected.

☆ To one side you glimpse a fissure in the rock, an opening from which comes a draught of cool, fresh sea air. You climb through the opening and find yourself in a vast cathedral-like cavern filled with a lake that you sense leads out of the mountain and spills into the sea.

☆ You enter the water and are carried by a warm current out of the mountain into the deepest depths of the ocean. Here dwell the creatures of the cold abyss. Rising higher towards the glittering sunlight on the surface you swim among the shoals of smaller fish, exotic plants and sculptured coral. Each creature is an indispensable element in the pattern of life.

☆ You rise up to the light and break the surface to emerge among the rocks, where the waves lap gently against the shoreline. Here amphibians reside in the world between water and air. Wading to shore, you watch the reptiles and insects moving in the marshes in the realm of weather and climate. Further inland is the moss on the rock, the trees and flowers in the valleys and on the hills. You see cattle grazing in the fields and birds migrating across sea and land. This is the hierarchy of nature.

☆ Now rise up and look down on the world from a great height. See humanity in all its variations: those who work with their hands, those who work in the realm of ideas, those who serve, those who learn and those who teach. See the villages, the towns and cities of the world bustling with humanity striving to survive and find meaning, value, dignity and purpose in their lives. See them growing, living, ageing and dying and the world they helped shaped and create moving inexorably on.

☆ Look beyond the physical, through the veil of the clouds, and become conscious of the realm of spirit, the formless dimension of discarnate spirits who are resting and learning between lives. Here are the planes which some call Heaven and Hell, where those of a like mind are drawn together. Consider what holds those in the Hell of their own making.

☆ Now ascend still higher to the place of the Elohim (see page 47) who watch over the spiritual progress of humanity. Above them rises the Throne of Heaven,

supported by the lion, the bull, the eagle and the man –
the symbols of the Four Worlds of Emanation,
Creation, Formation and Action and the four elements
within each: air, fire, water and earth. Surrounding
them are the myriads of angelic hosts overseeing
millions of cosmic processes.

☆ Rise higher still and come into the presence of the
primordial man, Adam Kadmon, the figure upon the
throne, who is the human image of the Divine. Know
that you are an indispensable cell of his being, the
flawless, blessed and beloved son or daughter of the
Divine. You and the Divine are indivisible. Separation is
an illusion. Bathe in the light and absorb whatever you
need at this moment in your life from the eternal light
of his being.

☆ When you are ready, gently descend from the Divine
dimension to the realm of physical reality. Pass the
planets of our solar system and draw near to the earth.
Descend through the clouds, pass over the oceans and
return to this country, this town, this room. Become
aware of your breathing, sense your body and become
aware of your surroundings. And, when you are ready,
open your eyes.

# 3

# The Four Worlds

'Even every one that is called by My Name; for I have created him for My Glory, I have formed him: yea I have made him.' – Isaiah 43:7.

Many scientists doubt the existence of the supernatural. They claim that if they cannot measure it, then it does not exist. But they are continually being forced to rewrite the rules of what is and is not possible to accommodate the latest discoveries, such as the manufacture of anti-matter or the anomalies of quantum theory. Some of the more visionary physicists now anticipate proof of the existence of other dimensions in our universe at a subatomic level within a few generations.

The vast majority of the general public, who are becoming increasingly fascinated by unusual or unexplained phenomena, are nevertheless reluctant to subscribe to something which they see as irrational and unpredictable. Though they are intrigued by phenomena that cannot be evaluated in scientific terms, they object to the fact that psychic phenomena appear to defy logic and the laws of the physical world. It is a paradox which only intrigues and confounds them further.

If the scientists and the sceptics were given access to any of the esoteric teachings which are at the heart of the major world religions, of which Kabbalah is but one, they would have a key to explore the greater and lesser mysteries for themselves. These reveal the existence of a greater reality that conforms to both universal and natural laws. It is a reflection of the physical world, whether those who live in it acknowledge it or not. In contrast, the ephemeral phenomena of the material world perpetuate the illusion that our physical dimension is the only reality.

## Jacob's Ladder

The Kabbalah offers a logical, holistic and harmonious system of perpetually unfolding creation – of four interdependent and interpenetrating worlds (multi-layered, overlapping worlds of increasingly dense matter), each containing the essence of the world from which it was generated. Collectively they are referred to as Jacob's Ladder in an allusion to Jacob's vision of the Ladder of Existence (see over). One of the best-known stories in the Old Testament tells how Jacob, the patriarch, dreamt of a ladder ascending to heaven.

### The World of Emanation

The World of Emanation (Azilut), traditionally symbolised by the element of fire, is the realm of perfection, of unity, beyond the finite dimensions of time and space. Here the laws and dynamics of creation wait upon the Divine will for, until the Divine presence manifests in existence, its potential is unfulfilled.

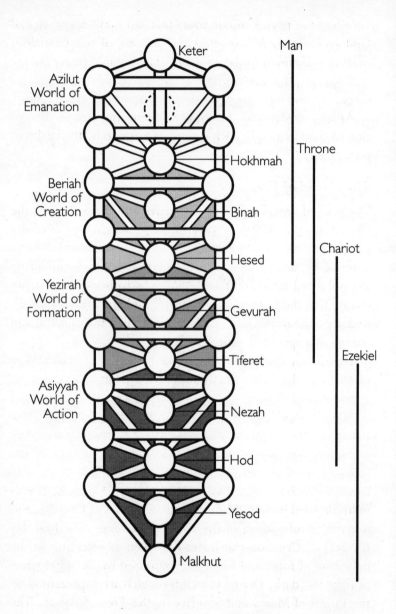

Jacob's Ladder – The Four Worlds

When the pure consciousness that we may choose to call God condensed, It instigated the process of manifestation, causing movement in the void and bringing into being energy and matter, the passive and active principles of form and force, and the dimensions of time and space.

Azilut translates as 'proximity', being the closest dimension to the Divine. As such it is considered to be the realm of pure spirit.

## The World of Creation

The second world in order of density and descent from the Divine is the World of Creation (Beriah) traditionally symbolised by the element of air. It is the realm of essence where form and force are brought into balance, harmonising the polarised male and female energies to bring order from chaos. It is the heaven of biblical mythology which is inhabited by the archangels, each personifying the quality and energy of a specific sephirah.

Here, too, dwell the evolved souls who have broken free of the wheel of life, death and rebirth, but who chose to continue to influence the spiritual progress of human kind from the world of spirit or by descent into the flesh. Here exists the bodhisattvas of the Buddhist tradition, the avatars worshipped by the Hindu and the Messianic figures of the Judeao-Christian tradition. It is the unfolding of this world from the heart centre (Tiferet) of the world above that is mythologised in the Old Testament as the act of Creation and not the manifestation of the physical universe. The first day (or act) of Creation can instead be seen as referring to the balancing of form and force as symbolised by the emergence of light and dark, Divine principles which are represented by the Pillars of Mercy and Severity on the Tree of Beriah. The second day, described in Genesis as the dividing of the

heavens between the waters above from those below, corresponds to the emergence of the upper triad on the Beriatic
Tree of Creation from the lower sephiroth of the Azilutic
Tree of Emanation. The following five days describe the
emergence of the remaining sephiroth in similar symbolic
terms.

## The World of Formation

The third world is the World of Formation (Yezirah) traditionally symbolised by the element of water. It is the world
of psychic phenomena which occultists call the astral plane. It
is the realm beyond waking consciousness, often penetrated
in our sleep and from which we return with our most vivid
dreams. It is also the first stage on our journey back to the
Creator after discarding the physical body at death. This is
where we find the Heaven and Hell of our own making, for
here thought creates the illusion of form.

Here too dwell the hierarchy of angelic hosts, discarnate
entities who were created as Divine intermediaries, whose
role is to ensure that the evolutionary impulse takes the form
designated by the will of God.

This is the plane of existence mythologised in the Old
Testament as the Garden of Eden, where the 'models' for the
various species were determined before incarnating in their
infinite variety in the fourth world, the World of Action, our
physical realm.

For centuries Bible scholars have considered the repetition
of the creative process in the second chapter of Genesis to be
a poetic indulgence on the part of the anonymous scribes. In
fact it describes the unfolding of Yezirah, the third world, as
shown by a subtle change of wording. Genesis 1:27 says: 'So
God created man' while Genesis 2:7 says 'And the Lord God
formed man'. As the renowned modern Kabbalist Z'ev ben

Shimon Halevi noted in one of his many books on the subject: 'There is literally a World of difference' between the words 'created' and 'formed'.

The use of different names for God is also highly significant. In Kabbalah the individual sephiroth are each assigned different God names to further define their qualities and characteristics. Therefore Elohim, the Hebrew name for God used in Genesis 1:27, and Yhvh Elohim, the name used in Genesis 2:7, again signify different stages in the process of the Divine descent into matter. Elohim is plural and as such denotes the coming together of two attributes to call forth Creation, whereas the composite name Yhvh Elohim translates as God the Creator, reflecting the idea that the World of Formation, emanated from the heart centre of the world above, the World of Creation. Elohim translates literally as 'many Gods' but in Kabbalistic terms it is understood as meaning 'I will be manifest in many'; so in one context it is a specific God name to denote a particular level at which God is manifest and in the other context it refers to the forms which God took.

## The World of Action

In describing the river which flowed out of the garden of Eden the Old Testament scribes were giving an account of the emergence of the fourth world, Asiyyah, the World of Action traditionally symbolised by the element of earth. Asiyyah emerged from the heart centre of Beriah, the astral world. The choice of imagery was intended to convey the idea that the astral world is the world of the emotions as symbolised by water.

The river that flowed out of Eden was said to have four heads indicating the four great stages of manifestation by which each of these worlds came into being, traditionally designated as Calling, Creating, Forming and Making. In terms of human endeavour the process can be seen to correspond with having the initial idea to make something, then creating a mental image to define whatever it is that we desire before we develop detailed plans or a model. Finally it takes a physical form based on the image in our imagination.

In a sense God created the four worlds in a process similar to that with which we create our own personal world, that is as a means of self-expression to reflect and define who we are. To the external world we project an image which is a crude reflection, emphasising only certain aspects of our personality, while to family and friends we appear truer to ourselves. To an intimate friend or partner we strip away all pretence, but only in our own company are we able to distinguish our personality (the behavioural and mental characteristics which make each individual unique) from our persona (the personality we assume to help us interact with the world). Even then it is only by withdrawing from the worlds of our own making and into ourselves that we get a real sense of who we truly are.

## Ezekiel's Vision and the Four Elements

As mentioned in Chapter 1, Kabbalah is understood to have developed from the Jewish mystical tradition known as Merkabah, or Work of the Chariot, whose origins are to be found in Ezekiel's vision. For the Kabbalist, the imagery Ezekiel describes is understood to be symbolic of the Four Worlds and of the elements within them.

The vision came to the prophet by the banks of River Cheber, where he saw what he described as a fiery chariot emerging from an amber cloud. It was drawn by four winged creatures, each with four faces; those of a man, a lion, an ox and an eagle. He compared the chariot to a blazing platform turning upon wheels within wheels in which rings of eyes were to be seen. 'And above the firmament that was over their heads was the likeness of a throne, as the appearance of a sapphire stone; and upon the likeness of the throne was a likeness as the appearance of a man upon it above.' Ezekiel 1:26.

From the repeated use of the Hebrew word '*demut*', which translates as 'likeness', it is clear that Ezekiel was stressing the symbolic nature of the images. As such, the human figure can be seen as representing Adam Kadmon, rather than God, as is commonly believed. This Divine man is surrounded by an aura, radiating all the colours of the rainbow, emphasising the idea that the energy emanating from the Divine manifests at different frequencies that we perceive visually as the various colours of the spectrum and, at a subtler level, as the corresponding colours of the chakras in the human aura.

The other elements of the vision represent the Worlds of Creation, Formation and Action and the four corresponding realms or levels within each of these. The throne symbolises the World of Creation, the chariot represents the World of Formation and Ezekiel stands in for man in the World of Action.

On the four-faced winged creatures, the man represents the primordial man in the World of Emanation and its corresponding element – fire. The eagle represents the World of Creation and its corresponding element – air. The lion represents the World of Formation, the realm of the heart and the emotions and its corresponding element – water. The bull represents the World of Action, with its corresponding element – earth.

## Macrocosmos and Microcosmos

When focused in the microcosmic image of man, the Four Worlds of Emanation, Creation, Formation and Action are seen to be the Divine equivalents of will, intellect, emotion and action.

All human beings inhabit these four dimensions of increasingly finite matter simultaneously, although most of us are not conscious of it. Our soul or will exists in the spiritual dimension, our consciousness in the realm of the intellect, our emotions in the astral dimension and the activities of our physical body in the dense World of Action.

While we spend most of our lives preoccupied with the concerns of the latter we drift in and out of the astral dimension during sleep whenever the astral or emotional body floats free of the physical. Unfortunately, our experience of the two higher worlds is largely limited to infrequent flashes of inspiration and the momentary glimpse of a greater reality which tradition assures us happens to every individual at least once in their lifetime. Kabbalah is concerned with developing a conscious awareness of each of the four worlds and the elements within them. Through Kabbalah we can cultivate a compassionate detachment to the physical world, exercise control over the emotional dimension and have a continual sense of the upper and interior worlds.

### Exercises: The Four Worlds

The following four exercises are designed to increase your awareness and understanding of the four worlds and the levels within each of them. It is advisable to perform each exercise separately on different days, taking about 15 minutes for each one. Once you feel comfortable and familiar with them they can be combined to create a 'Grand Tour' of the various levels of consciousness and creation. In any event, you are urged to begin your meditation with the basic grounding exercise.

## ASIYYAH, THE WORLD OF ACTION

☆ Make yourself comfortable in a chair or, if you prefer, lie on a mat on the floor or on a bed. Close your eyes and begin by focusing on your breathing. Take slow, deep regular breaths and with each exhalation feel the tension dissolve and leave your muscles, beginning with those in your head and ending with your toes. With each inhalation, imagine that you are breathing in an intoxicating incense with the power to fully relax you while clarifying your mind.

☆ Now visualise yourself standing in a forest clearing before a blacksmith's forge. Look across to the mountains in the far distance. Imagine how it must be to gaze upon such a view in search of inspiration.

☆ You look about you, but as there is no one to be seen you draw closer to examine the tools and the finished examples of the blacksmith's work which hang from the rafters.

☆ The blacksmith appears and greets you as if he has been expecting you for some time. He offers to make a personalised amulet for you, something which symbolises your true inner nature and which will be uniquely yours. He looks at you with the eyes of someone who can see right through to the soul and then makes a rough sketch of the design. What does he draw? Perhaps it is a symbol of your Higher Self, of your purpose in this life or your particular strengths.

☆ Observe with interest as he then begins to shovel the raw material into the furnace and pump the bellows until the minerals are consumed in the flames. After a few moments he draws the molten metal from the fire and pours it into a mould. It cools in seconds. As you watch, he taps the blackened lump of metal out and carries it across to his anvil with a pair of tongs. There, with his hammer, he works it for a few moments, fashioning the final shape until it is finished to his satisfaction. See the sparks fly, feel the heat of the furnace, hear the clang of metal on metal and smell the metallic essence on the air.

☆ Finally he grips the amulet between a pair of tongs and plunges it into a bucket of water, filling the forge with steam. When the steam clears he takes it to his bench and attaches a small chain so that you can hang it around your neck.

☆ With pride he hands it to you and now you can see it in detail. Take a long look at it and thank him for this gift.

☆ Now imagine the scene fading as you feel yourself being drawn back into your body. Become aware of your surroundings. When you are ready, open your eyes.

In subsequent meditations the gift you will be given may alter. It is likely to be a symbol of your current stage of awareness or of something you need to move on to the next phase of your life.

## YEZIRAH, THE WORLD OF FORMATION

This exercise will be greatly enhanced by the addition of some gentle background music.

☆ Begin by relaxing and focusing on your breath.

☆ When you are ready, visualise yourself in a beautiful garden which slopes gently down to a lake. In the centre of the lake is a large island on which stands a small white temple of classical design.

☆ You walk through the garden towards the shore of the lake, where a boat is moored, waiting to take you across to the island. But as you cross the lawn you slow down to watch a group of people on the right resting in the sun. Some appear to be asleep, others are strolling among the flowerbeds, enjoying the scent of the flowers. At first sight it appears an idyllic picture, but you sense that something is missing.

☆ You then become aware of sweet, enchanting music, drifting on the breeze from the direction of the island. These people seem completely oblivious to it.

☆ On your left is another group, dressed far too warmly for the hot weather and engaged in heavy digging, which they seem to bitterly resent. They stand in a huge circle, wiping the sweat from their brows, cursing silently to themselves and glancing furtively over their shoulders at what you sense are imaginary overseers. As one digs out a spadeful of earth their neighbour fills it with soil from their own hole, so their work is purposeless and neverending.

☆ These two groups are in the Heaven and Hell of their own making. Both, in their own way, are content to be where they expected to find themselves.

☆ But once again you are entranced by the music drifting in on the air and are eager to find its source. You sense that there is more to be discovered on the island and that this garden is only the first stage in a far longer journey.

☆ You walk down to the lakeside and climb into the boat. What kind of boat is it? Is it in good repair? You make the crossing to the island. Is it smooth sailing, or do you find yourself drifting and struggling against the current?

☆ You finally arrive at the island, whose foliage and animal life are more exotic and colourful than any found on earth. You moor the boat and move inland, where you find a group of people enjoying themselves in various forms of creative work. A small ensemble is playing the music that you have heard ever since your arrival in the garden. You do not recognise it, but it is strangely familiar and strengthens the feeling you have of coming home to a place where you truly belong. Curiously they are not playing from a score but appear to be improvising in perfect harmony, drawing inspiration from their surroundings.

☆ Other people are engaged in painting, dancing, perfecting physical disciplines such as tai chi and yoga and rehearsing the roles that they will play when they return to the World of Action from which you came.

☆ As you listen to the music you sense a warm glow in your solar plexus, the emotional centre. It seems to grow as the music envelops you. You dissolve into the music. The solar plexus centre softens, the glow blossoming like a white lotus in the pit of your stomach, releasing healing light to every cell of your being. Bathe in the glow and let the music be the wings that lift you higher and higher to touch the source of your being.

☆ When you are ready, come gently back into your body. Count slowly down from ten to one, visualising the energy centres from crown to ground in the body as you do so. Then become aware of your surroundings, and open your eyes.

## BERIAH, THE WORLD OF CREATION

☆ Begin by relaxing and focusing on your breath.

☆ Now visualise yourself in the entrance hall of a vast library. Let the image come to mind and the detail develop of its own accord, as if it was a picture developing on a sheet of photographic paper.

☆ When you are ready, walk through into the main chamber, which is stacked high with every book that has ever been printed. Perhaps you find it as a musty room, dimly lit and overcrowded with well thumbed volumes of archaic knowledge. Or perhaps you find yourself in a spacious, well-lit modern building, where gallery upon gallery of chromium shelves rise to a white, domed ceiling.

☆ Is your library a place where secrets are stored in safe keeping exclusively for the initiated, or is it a public place of learning where all have access to the latest theories and discoveries? You would like more time to explore and browse among the shelves, but this can wait for a subsequent visit. Now you feel compelled to explore the interior workings of the building to find out how all this knowledge came to be here and for what purpose.

☆ You climb the stairs to the first floor and follow a sign to a small room, set to one side. There you find a number of craftsmen repairing the bindings of old, cracked, leatherbound volumes with great care, skill and patience. On the other side of the wall, in the next room, you can hear the clatter of printing presses. The door between the two rooms is flung open and another stack of freshly printed books is brought in to be collated and bound. You sense that there is a ready and eager readership waiting for both in the outside world.

☆ You walk out of the room and climb the stairs to the second floor, where you follow a sign to another side-room. Here you find a group of illustrators sketching covers for new titles and finalising the lettering to be used. Although they must have done this a thousand times, you sense that they have never tired of their task, but take a great personal pride in their work. Across the room another group is selecting the paper and the leather binding to be used for particular titles.

✩ You leave the room and walk up to the third floor. Here you find another group, annotating the texts with their own comments, condensing long passages and clarifying the arguments. They too seem unhurried, proud to be making their contribution to the spread of knowledge.

✩ Finally you climb to the fourth floor, where there are no shelves of books. In their place a thousand scribes sit in meditation before a vast embroidered curtain, veiling the Holy of Holies. From time to time the scribes break off their meditation to transcribe what they have received. Here the presence of God is overwhelming. In the silence and serenity of this chamber you too receive something of great significance intuitively. What is it?

✩ Now is the time to return to the ground floor. You descend the four flights of stairs. Just as you are leaving the head librarian calls you by name. He or she comes over to you and, smiling broadly, hands you two books. One is a restored volume which you had seen being repaired and the other is a new title. You look at the covers and sense that they are the right books for you at this particular moment in your life. What are they? If the titles or cover illustrations do not come readily to mind, do not worry about it. They may come in your dreams or when you are next in need of guidance or inspiration.

✩ You turn to thank the librarian, but he or she has gone. You leave the library and return to your body. Become aware once again of your surroundings, sense your body and, when you are ready, open your eyes.

## Azilut, the World of Emanation

☆ Begin by relaxing and focusing on your breath.

☆ Now visualise yourself at the base of a high and imposing mountain. It is night and the stars glisten above you in the infinity of space. Feel the crisp, clean air on your face and the firmness of the earth beneath your feet.

☆ You are going to climb the mountain without equipment of any sort, for there is something to be learned in the ascent and more to be discovered at the summit. Instead you will have the assistance of a guide who knows every foothold, ledge and sheltering spot and in whose company you are guaranteed a safe journey to the summit and back. Your guide is unlike any other you may have encountered for this is a unique journey to the summit of your own consciousness.

☆ The guide now appears before you. Your guide has a serenely beautiful face and gives the impression of being both a powerful protector and a loving friend. Nevertheless, do not hesitate to test for deception by saying a prayer, sacred phrase or uttering any of the Divine names listed on page 83. If the image is false it will break up and fade.

☆ When you have a constant image, proceed. Although your guide goes before you, as you begin your ascent you have the sense that you alone are determining the direction and pace. Your footholds are firm and secure and your progress is swift and exhilarating.

☆ You pass through a cloud bank, all the time keeping a close watch on your guide who is only a few metres ahead of you. When you emerge on the other side the air seems more rarefied and your head is clearer. You continue your ascent, resisting the urge to look back or to either side, although you might hear the sounds of animals some distance away.

☆ Eventually the sky begins to lighten and the summit comes into view. It is a magnificent sight. You pause for a moment struck by its immensity and a real sense of the power that fashioned it. You, too, are part of that same creative force and now you are ascending to a place where you know you will make contact with the source.

☆ You have a sense of excitement and anticipation as the sun rises over the mountain peak setting its ragged outline into silhouette.

☆ In a few moments you will stand before something for which you have been searching a long time. You scramble up the last few feet to a vast plateau, seemingly without end. You have the sense of being on the roof of the world. Above you the sky is a mix of fiery hues, a firmament of elemental energies. It is as if you are seeing the forces behind nature for the first time.

☆ Your guide beckons you forward to a stone altar between two mighty pillars. On the altar you find that which you seek. What is it?

☆ Whether it is a traditional symbol of the quest such

as the Holy Grail or an object of personal significance, know that it reflects your true nature. And know, too, that in making this ascent you are expressing your will to meet with your Higher Self. It is certain to respond.

☆ When you are ready, thank your guide and begin your descent down the mountain taking the object of your quest with you.

☆ When you find yourself back on the ground gradually become aware again of your surroundings and the seat you are sitting in. Then, when you are ready, open your eyes.

(If you wish, this exercise can form the first part of a longer and more powerful visualisation when combined with the exercise Angels of the Sephiroth in Chapter 5.)

# 4

# Man the Microcosm

'The Holy One, blessed be He, made man by printing the image of the kingdom of heaven within him, which is the image of the All. It is this image which the Holy One, blessed be He, beheld when he made the world and all the creatures of the world. This image is the synthesis of all creatures above and all creatures below, with no separation; it is the synthesis of all the sephiroth, all their names, all their epithets and all their denominations' – *Sefer ha Zohar*.

The following sections are presented in a logical sequence so that you can see how the Tree of Life and its principles operate at various levels in the real world and in your personal lives.

## Adam Kadmon

In the Judaeo-Christian tradition we are told that man was created in the image of God. This is clearly implausible as God must possess the essence of both male and female aspects and transcend the limits of form.

Kabbalists contend that the universe and everything within it is a reflection of God, but His existence is expressed in an infinite variety of physical forms and therefore it must be the essence, or the spirit, of living things which mirrors the Divine source. For that reason, when Kabbalists describe human beings as descendants of an androgynous primordial cosmic being known as Adam Kadmon, they are speaking metaphorically of the original blueprint or model of a human being. It was projected from the mind of God in increasingly finite and detailed form through the higher worlds before manifesting in its separate male and female aspects in our physical world.

The mythical Adam described in the Book of Genesis is an allusion to the refined models inhabiting the Worlds of Creation and Formation. The so-called Fall is a veiled reference to the awakening of our sensual nature in the descent from the World of Formation to the physical World of Action for which we acquired our 'coats of skin'.

Kabbalists contend that we were all once an indivisible part of Adam Kadmon in Azilut, the World of Emanation. While our souls remain on that level our mental, emotional and physical bodies became, in effect, separated cells in our descent through the lower worlds. However, this sense of separation is an illusion. Only those who have experienced mystical union with the source while still in the body can begin to understand it. For the majority of people such concepts are a paradox, yet it is easily explained by the fact that our consciousness is not limited by the form in which we find ourselves. However, our understanding is limited by our intellect.

## The Cycle of Life

Our personal descent through the Four Worlds is completed with the acquisition of a physical body which serves as the soul's vehicle for experiencing the mineral, vegetable, animal and human realms of the World of Action.

In this world we learn to cope with a body which is composed of minerals and which needs nourishment to sustain itself and propagate the species as part of a vegetable-like process. We also learn to survive on our instincts and interact with others as the animals do. The human or Divine aspect of man finds expression in the intellect and also in reflection, compassion and an insatiable curiosity concerning his origins and destiny.

Our unconscious impulse to evolve and return to the source is seen in the cycle of life and death, which follows the order of the sephiroth on the Tree of Life in reverse. As an embryo we are preoccupied solely with physical growth, sustenance and comfort, and are therefore centred and grounded in Malkhut. As a baby we ascend to Yesod, developing an ego, while childhood corresponds to the defining nature of Hod as we learn about ourselves and the world in which we live. Youth is characterised by intense activity and instinctive responses are represented by Nezah, the next sephirah in the order of ascent, while maturity brings self-awareness, symbolised by Tiferet.

At this stage we have the free will to go further and develop self-knowledge, or merely to ricochet between the lower sephiroth like a stray ball in a pinball machine, gratifying the senses at Nezah, indulging the intellect in the manipulative games of Hod, massaging the ego in Yesod and grasping at the empty symbols of materialism at Malkhut. People of power and influence, such as politicians, academics, scientists, union leaders, businessmen and some religious leaders, owe their position to the development of self-will at Tiferet, but either they lack the imagination to look beyond their sphere of influence or they are undermined by imbalances in the lower sephiroth before they can attempt the ascent.

Beyond the levels of Nezah, Hod, Yesod and Malkhut a person reaches the level of self-awareness and enlightenment of a Buddha or Christ etc – a fully-realised human being.

Many of the most significant figures in history have found that, while ambition and self-will enabled them to scramble up the lower portion of the Tree to positions of power and influence, a reckless disregard for personal development can leave the lower sephiroth undeveloped resulting in an excess of animal passions, an inflated ego and a Machiavellian belief that somehow they will deny these universal laws and get away with it.

If, instead, we choose to develop beyond what amounts to the vegetable and animal states we have to ensure that our footholds on the lower portion of the Tree are secure before we can climb higher in search of self-knowledge.

## The Sephirotic Stages of the Nation

Nations too, evolve through the identifiable stages on the cycle of life, developing according to the configuration of the sephiroth and even getting stuck at key points, just as people do. Recognising these stages of development helps to put the history of a country into perspective. It can also explain why the leaders of a particular country took a certain action and it can even help to predict how they are likely to react in a future crisis.

A nation's embryonic stage is marked by its formation from a number of separate states or kingdoms into a single nation. Its infant stage occurs when it seeks to establish a separate identity and a sense of self, usually when it plunders its own resources to build its infrastructure and establish its boundaries. The next stage is the equivalent of childhood, in which the leaders of the nation attempt to extend their boundaries and influence, often resulting in conflict with other nations. Unless a neighbouring nation assumes the role of parent or policeman, Justice (Gevurah) – balancing it with Mercy (Hesed) when doing so – to re-establish the emerging nation's physical and behavioural boundaries, it is in danger of becoming the neighbourhood bully.

Nations which develop beyond this point often find themselves making the mistakes of youth. They will assert their rights, as they see them, without considering the feelings or rights of others, and think of themselves unfairly criticised for having done so, as the Israelis discovered after invading Lebanon in 1982. They will assume that their well-intentioned efforts to right the wrongs of the world will be appreciated and rewarded, but will discover that life is harsh, unpredictable, cruel and capricious, as the United States found to their cost after blundering into Vietnam in the 1960s. Later it will inevitably discover that even its parents (or leaders) are not infallible, as the Watergate scandal of 1973 proved to the disbelief of American citizens. The nation will then move on to the cynicism or resignation of adulthood, in which its own welfare and self-preservation are paramount as it re-evaluates its view of the world, its responsibilities and its place in that world. With middle age comes maturity and a degree of self-awareness. This is the stage which corresponds to Tiferet, at which the nation can develop self-will, rising above petty squabbles, self-interest and the other manifestations of immaturity which mark an undeveloped and unbalanced personality. If the nations ever reached full maturity this would achieve the ultimate aim of manifesting Heaven on Earth.

Of course, a nation's destiny is also determined by many other factors, including external influences and the self-will of individuals from within. Astrological influences, for example, are another factor to be taken into consideration when determining a nation's development, as each is under the influence of cosmic forces, as are individuals. As an example, Germany was formed from a confederation of separate states in 1871, which brought it under the influence of Scorpio, whose characteristics include the vices of gross egotism, seductiveness, abuse of trust and the inability to understand others or leave the past behind. These vices or negative attributes of the sephiroth were ruthlessly exploited by Hitler and the Nazi regime in the 1920s and 1930s, before the balance was restored at horrific cost to humanity.

However, at any point in a nation's history it has the free will to draw strength from a critical situation and overcome its inherent weaknesses, as Germany did after the war. It was forced to collectively acknowledge its shadow self and draw instead on its corresponding strengths, which include the assimilation of grief, self-healing and acceptance of the need for transformation, change and rebirth.

This oversimplifies the way Kabbalistic principles operate in the field of astrology, but it is sufficient to be aware that vices and virtues operate in ourselves as individuals, as well as in larger communities.

## The Sephiroth and the Chakras

It is not coincidental that, when overlaid on the human body, the configuration of the sephiroth roughly corresponds with the chakras, or subtle energy centres of Eastern philosophy, for all true traditions share the same fundamental truths.

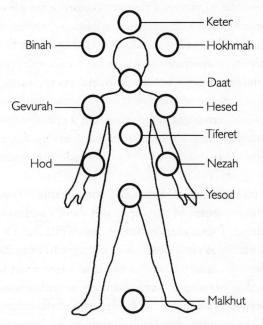

The sephiroth as placed on the human body, psyche and spirit

Keter, the Crown, corresponds to the Crown chakra, visualised as just above the head with Hokhmah (Wisdom) and
Binah (Understanding) placed over the brain at the level of
the Third Eye chakra. Daat, the unmanifest sephiroth of
Higher Knowledge, is traditionally envisaged as covering the
face and throat as the focal energy centre for sight, sound,
smell and speech, functions otherwise attributed to the
Throat chakra. Gevurah (Judgement) and Hesed (Mercy) are
placed to the right and left of the heart centre, with Tiferet
(Beauty) corresponding to the Solar Plexus chakra, the seat
of the emotions. In Kabbalistic meditation the qualities of this
last sephirah can begin to be experienced by softening the

Solar Plexus chakra with suitable music, contemplating natural beauty or the remembrance of intense feelings. Hod (Reverberation), Nezah (Eternity) and Yesod (Foundation) form a triad around the area of influence, corresponding to the Sacral chakra, while Malkhut (Kingdom) corresponds to the Base chakra at the feet.

As a reflection of the image of Adam Kadmon the arms and legs are seen as corresponding to the outer active and passive Pillars of Mercy and Severity, with the spine as the central Pillar of Equilibrium.

## EXERCISE: THE MIDDLE PILLAR

This exercise was developed by Israel Regardie, a founder member of the Hermetic Order of the Golden Dawn, to illustrate the correspondence between the sephiroth as they relate to the human body and the chakras. Its aim is to balance the energy centres in the body, clear emotional blockages and aid the free flow of energy around the body. If practised regularly it should bring a greater sense of well-being and improved health. It is recommended that you sit in a chair with your feet flat on the floor and hands on your thighs.

☆ Begin by closing your eyes and focusing on your breath. You could utter a prayer of devotion or dedication of your own choosing to help still the mind and raise your level of awareness.

☆ When you feel relaxed, begin by visualising a luminous white light of vibrant energy above your head. This is the Crown sephirah, the Divine source from which you need to draw energy. As you visualise it, repeat the Divine name Eheieh (Eh-Huh-Yeh) associated with this sphere, until you can feel the presence of a concentration of energy above your head. Now imagine the light descending through the top of your head to activate the Third Eye chakra in the middle of your forehead between the brows. Sense it pulsing, filling your head with light as you repeat the Divine name Eheieh.

☆ Then visualise the light entering and revitalising the other energy centres. As you imagine them intone the Divine names associated with each: the throat, Yhvh Elohim (pronounced Jah-ho-vah Elo-heem); the heart, Yhvh Eloah VaDaath (Jah-ho-vah Elo-a Va-Dat); the groin, Shadda El Chai (Sha-die El Chi); and the feet, Adonai Ha-Aretz (Ado-nigh Ha Erets). Feel the energy shining at each sphere and in a continual shaft of light, connecting them from the crown to the feet.

☆ Now exhale slowly and perceive the energy flow back up into the crown, until it overflows from the crown and cascades down your left-hand side radiating outward to energise the aura.

☆ Then inhale slowly, drawing energy up the right side of the body and radiating outward to the aura on that side. Repeat this until you feel the warmth of the circulating energy.

☆ Now exhale and imagine the energy cascading from the crown, down the front of your body, and draw it up behind you from heel to crown as you inhale.

☆ Finally, allow the energy to gather at the foot centre.

As you inhale slowly draw it up to the crown, letting it overflow as you exhale. Bask in the shower of light and energy droplets. Repeat as often as you like.

☆ End the exercise by closing down the energy centres, perhaps by visualising them as folding lotus flowers of various colours. Ground yourself by stamping your feet to bring yourself back to earth.

## The Tree of Psyche

It can be seen that the upper portion of the Tree corresponds to the realm of the collective unconscious, the central segment which overlaps at Daat is the dimension of the individual unconscious and the lower part which overlaps at Tiferet corresponds to personal consciousness.

On the Tree of the Psyche the exterior passive and active pillars are renamed the Pillars of Structure and Dynamic. At this level Keter now corresponds to the soul or Higher Self, from which we derive flashes of insight and inspiration. These communications come either by grace or as a result of attaining an altered state of consciousness in contemplation or meditation. They are channelled through Daat, the unmanifest sephirah, which can be visualised as the veil which separates us from our Higher Self.

Moving down the Tree of the Psyche, the first sephirah on the Pillar of Structure is Binah (Understanding), which at this level expresses the passive and reflective function of the intellect in the quality of contemplation. It is balanced on the Pillar of Dynamic by Hokhmah (Wisdom), the quality of revelation which is the expression of the active inner intellect. In practical terms, balancing these two sephiroth involves consideration of all the consequences before acting on intuition. At another level it emphasises the interdependence of revelation and reflection as identifiable stages in the process of forming opinions, attitudes and a personal philosophy.

The first of the three sephiroth corresponding to the emotions is Gevurah (Judgement), which represents the qualities of discipline and decision-making and is the seat of the superego or conscience. It could be envisaged as our own internal policeman, reminding us of our duties and responsibilities and endeavouring to make us act on our better instincts. When balanced by the quality encapsulated in Hesed (Mercy), it can drive us to work hard and adhere to the moral and civil laws of our society. If we allow Gevurah free rein in our own psyche we become intolerant of imperfections in ourselves and others, and may find ourselves chained to our jobs or our chores when we should be enjoying the rewards of hard work. It is not uncommon to find that people who drive themselves mercilessly are equally demanding of others and that in being fastidious or hard on themselves they alienate their colleagues, family and friends without realising that what was once a virtue has become, in effect, a vice.

For every attribute there is a positive and a negative aspect which we can equate with the traditional vices and virtues. If we strike the balance right the complementary attributes assume the quality of virtues, but if we favour one at the expense of the other, one will become overemphasised and the other neglected. Both are then corrupted and assume the aspect of the traditional vices.

In an individual an imbalance of these two sephiroth would lead either to indecision if the imbalance was in favour of Mercy, or to stifling self-criticism and crippling self-consciousness if the swing leaned towards Judgement. An imbalance of the same sephiroth could result in either

fastidiousness or slovenliness in the individual, whereas the quality we should be aiming for between being overly critical on the one hand and too casual on the other is discernment.

At a community or state level, an overemphasis of Judgement without due regard for Mercy will develop a draconian judicial system in which petty offences will be punished by disproportionately severe sentences and where capital punishment may become the ultimate expression of a state which has assumed the role of the Almighty. If the emphasis leans too much towards Mercy it would lead to an extremely lenient and indulgent judicial system, so obsessed with being seen to be fair to offenders that it loses sight of its obligations and responsibilities towards citizens or victims.

In descending the Tree of the Psyche, next comes Hod (Reverberation), which represents the cognitive and controlling psychobiological processes which control and limit the generative impulses. Balancing this is Nezah (Eternity), which corresponds to the instinctive and impulsive psychobiological processes governing the processes of growth and renewal. Below these lies the ego, or conscious mind, at Yesod. This sephirah is both generative and reflective, creating the image we have of ourselves and the mask or persona that we project outwardly to the world. This is the focal point through which we perceive the physical world. It is also the level at which we execute our will.

The Tree of the Psyche is ultimately grounded in the central nervous system of the physical body.

## The Physical Tree

'One man is equivalent to all Creation. One man is a World in miniature.' – Abot de Rabbi Nathan, 2nd century CE.

The validity of the Tree as a symbolic glyph is best appreciated when the Kabbalist applies the principles and structure to other aspects of existence. You only fully appreciate the theory if you try to apply it to something for yourself. As a final example, your exploration of the Tree can continue with an examination of the physical body.

The Four Worlds, existing as will, intellect, emotion and action, equate within us with the intellectual, electrical, chemical and mechanical processes in the physical body. The pillars of Force and Form can be renamed Energy and Matter, which are governed by the central Pillar of Consciousness. Keter can be seen as the brain. Binah and Hokhmah correspond to the voluntary and involuntary pyschobiological processes. Gevurah and Hesed equate to the anabolic and catabolic processes concerning the assimilation and release of energy. Hod and Nezah represent the monitoring and motoring systems (the clinical terms for the communication and mobility systems). Tiferet corresponds to the central nervous system and Yesod to the autonomic one. Malkhut, being the lowest point of manifestation, represents the region of the senses and our contact with the physical world.

## EXERCISE: THE ELEMENTS WITHIN

This exercise can be done sitting or lying down. If you are sitting have your back straight with your feet flat on the floor and slightly apart. Hands on your thighs.

☆ Close your eyes and begin by focusing on your breath. Take slow, deep, regular breaths. Consider this as the gaseous, or air, element of your being. Imagine that you are breathing out tension with every exhalation, and breathing in a warm, calming light with every inhalation.

☆ Now become aware of your bones, which support you and give your body form. Consider this to be the earthly element of your being.

☆ Now visualise the blood pumping around your body. This is the physical manifestation of the vital force which is revitalising each and every cell and carries oxygen to the vital organs. Consider this as the watery element of your being.

☆ Now extend your awareness an inch or so outside of your physical body and sense, or see with the inner eye the light blue outline of the aura. After a few moments visualise this blue outline being suffused with other vibrant colours as the aura expands with your increasing awareness. Consider this as the fiery element of your being.

☆ The inner eye, commonly known as the third eye, is the eye of the soul. With it you can explore the inner dimensions of your being and the worlds of the spirit. It is located in the centre of your forehead between the eyebrows. Focus on that place now, and sense the opening of the eye, which may begin as a tickling sensation. You may see a single eye glaring at you. If so, try and hold the image. When it first appears it can be disconcerting, but it is the first sign of your psychic awakening and its appearance in this symbolic form will help you to accept the Kabbalistic concept of yourself as a multi-dimensional being. Consider it as a manifestation of the Kabbalistic concept of Divine reflection: 'I Am That I Am.'

☆ Now become conscious of the vegetable principle within you which needs the four elements in the form of nourishment, light, air and water to grow, regenerate itself, and bear fruit.

☆ Then focus on the animal principle within, its instinct, vitality, curiosity, cunning, moods, sociability and mobility.

☆ Finally, sense the human aspect of your being – your memory, imagination, invention, reflection and the ability to expand consciousness beyond the physical dimension.

☆ Focus once again on the four elements of your physical body, on the heat in your skin, the air in your lungs, the blood in your veins and the bones which support your limbs and give you form. Now become aware of your surroundings, the chair that you are sitting in or the mat or bed that you are lying on, and open your eyes.

# 5

# The Higher Mysteries: A Kabbalistic Cosmology

'In the name of the Lord God of Israel, may Michael, the protection of God, be at my right hand, and Gabriel, the power of God, at my left, before me Uriel, the light of God, behind me Raphael, the healing of God, and above my head Shekhinat El, the presence of God.' – Jewish children's prayer.

It is not possible to give hard facts concerning the beings of other dimensions. I have gone further than many other writers/teachers in giving the principles and possibilities which govern these invisible realms. The reader must be left to test the truth of what follows for themselves.

## Inhabitants of the Inner Worlds

The ancient hermetic axiom which states 'As above, so below' is a perfect summary of the Kabbalistic concept of existence. It implies that the seemingly infinite variety of life in our physical world is reflected in a corresponding hierarchy of discarnate lifeforms in the inner and upper worlds.

If this is so, it would explain the existence and nature of the supernatural creatures who have haunted visionaries through the ages and appeared in the hallucinations of those whose sensory perception has been altered by drugs, alcohol or mental instability. It would also give a new perspective to our more vivid dreams and nightmares, for all these experiences are brief, distorted glimpses of the inner and upper worlds resulting from an altered state of consciousness. And by the term 'inner and upper worlds' I include the dark, uncharted realms of the unconscious. These experiences would be far less disturbing and incomprehensible if we could attain an altered state of consciousness at will, enabling us to distinguish between a real experience of the inner worlds and those images which are only a projection of our own fears or fantasies.

Kabbalah aims to prepare the initiate for these potentially enlightening and sometimes unsettling experiences through study and meditation, but even a maggid, an experienced teacher of the tradition, must test for deception at every stage, for the real demons are those created by the human mind. And these are frightening enough! Someone who has advanced far along the path has to be even more diligent as the most insidious form of deceit is self-deception.

The history of occult practice is littered with examples of men and women who accumulated considerable knowledge but little understanding. One only has to look at the childish antics – widely publicised in-fighting, obsession with acquiring titles to denote their status within the organisation and general egotistical power games – of self-centred eccentrics such as Aleister Crowley and S. L. MacGregor Mathers, to name but two, for proof of that. But no one is immune from the corrupting influence of their inner demons. Rabbi Maimonides, one of the most learned Talmudic scholars, is known to have ordered the burning of a mystical text, the *Shiur Komah*, because its allegorical description of God offended his Orthodox sensibilities.

It is a sobering fact that the greater progress one makes in Kabbalah, or any other spiritual discipline, the greater will be the efforts of the ego to reassert itself as the centre of its own universe. It will remind the meditator of more pleasurable ways to spend their time and it may even raise doubts as to the validity of the teachings by drawing attention to the fact that the vast majority of the human race appears to survive without sitting in silent contemplation or studying things it can't actually prove to be real. However, as practice and experience will reveal, the inner life is more real than the transient pleasures of the physical world. The apparent contentment of our more materialistic fellow citizens is really no more than the bliss of ignorance.

For good reason meditators have likened the conscious mind to a restless monkey, although an equally valid analogy might be to that of the mythical figure of Satan, the tempter.

## *Angels and Demons*

Of all lifeforms, above and below, humans alone have the capacity of free will. Even the angels do not possess it. That is why they do not intervene in human affairs unless called upon to do so, consciously or unconsciously. They are Divine intermediaries, hence their name, derived from the Greek word '*angelo*', meaning messenger (*malakh* in Hebrew). Free will is the exclusive attribute of human beings, who also happen to be the highest form of life in the physical world, the one world where action brings concrete results. This gives us a unique responsibility to aid the process of evolution and integration or pursue self-interest thereby empowering the contrary impulse of stagnation and inertia.

It is my personal understanding that the hierarchy of discarnate beings that inhabit the inner and upper worlds are neither benign nor malevolent by nature. They simply exist, as incomplete non-physical lifeforms in the process of 'becoming' in the great chain of evolution. As with wild animals, these beings are not evil as such, but they should nevertheless be avoided if encountered in meditation or during an out-of-body experience. After all, a lion is not a malicious beast, but you wouldn't think of poking one with a stick out of idle curiosity! Judaic tradition contends that evil is the negative principle which was brought into being when God discarded His earlier attempts to create the universe. Known as the *qliphot* (Hebrew for 'shells'), these are empty husks of what might have been. Their imperfect or demonic inhabitants are seen as a distortion of the Divine reflection and as such they constitute a contrary force to universal evolution.

## The Nature of Evil

Many modern Kabbalists still hold to the belief in a hierarchy of angels overseeing a myriad of cosmic processes while a host of demons vainly attempt to undermine their efforts, but I personally cannot reconcile the idea of evil existing as a conscious and wilful entity in a universe that is a reflection of a perfect, loving God.

Surely that which is perfect cannot create something which is imperfect. Therefore what we perceive as evil must be something which is unconscious of its Divine nature and temporarily insensitive to its influence. Thus evil, for want of a better term, only exists in the lower worlds because of its separation from the source.

In the higher World of Emanation, Azilut, for example, evil is merely a contrary impulse, the force of contraction attempting to contain the momentum of an eternally unfolding universe. In the denser world of Beriah, the World of Creation, it is the impulse for destruction and disintegration, although not in the sense that we understand those terms, for what is eternal cannot be destroyed, only reconstituted. In the astral dimension, Yezirah, the World of Formation, evil takes the form of negative emotions which harm no one but those who projected them into this dimension.

If we have hateful thoughts we poison our entire system, which can result in ill health and mental instability. If you doubt the power of the mind to influence the body and the psyche, consider the number of resentful, frustrated and embittered people who look as if they are enjoying or even benefiting from their anger! If a person persists in empowering the negative aspects of their nature, or enslaves themselves through addiction or an obsession of any kind, they will unconsciously be creating a thought form in the astral dimension. It will suck their vitality during life and may also make it difficult for them to discard their astral body after death. If this occurs, their ascent to the higher worlds will be delayed until they become conscious both of the fact that they are 'dead' and that they are giving succour to something which is essentially alien to their divine nature.

Another contemporary Kabbalist, Z'ev ben Shimon Halevi, contends that evil is of our own making, the highest form of which is self-will. This is the principle personified in the myth of Lucifer, the angel who fell from grace through his own pride and arrogance. Another manifestation would be any form of inequality between individuals or groups of people. Inequality results from an imbalance of the Divine attributes and is contrary to the will of God, who is the father of all. A third aspect of evil takes the form of death, decay and disintegration, which are not evil if perceived as being merely the recycling stages in the natural processes of life.

The non-existence of evil as a separate malevolent force seems to be confirmed by the fact that evil can only be defined in our physical world in terms of inhuman acts carried out by one person against another. Despite claims to the contrary, there has never been any proof that aggressive acts are inspired by agencies other than the perpetrator's own will to destroy the life that God granted to all. This wilful desire to take the life of another, or to devalue that life in any way, is surely the true meaning of evil.

According to Kabbalistic tradition angelic beings are aiding the Divine process of evolution – angelic encounters are surprisingly widespread even among non-religious or non-spiritually-minded people – however, it does not follow that there must be demons. The word demon is a corruption of the Greek word *daimon* meaning 'spirit' or 'deity'. Certainly, the Kabbalah conceives of dual impulses and attributes with negative and positive aspects, but no one has been able to prove the existence of demons. If we need to balance the angelic forces with a contrary impulse, then would it not make sense to have the shadow side of human nature assume that role, for are not most of us in denial of our Divine nature? Are we not, therefore, the fallen angels and demons that we once feared?

## Satan, the Tempter

Judaism is suffused with superstition. The fear of tempting fate or of incurring the wrath of an angry, omnipotent God is ingrained in its customs, religious rituals and teachings, despite the fact that, through the centuries Jews have had more reason to fear persecution from their human neighbours than from supernatural forces.

Ironically, Jews do not actually believe in evil as a conscious force or the Devil as its malevolent personification. The Devil appears to have been a creation of the ascetic Essenes, who needed a symbol to embody the thoughts and actions that they considered contrary to the will of God. When certain of their number joined the radical Rabbi Jesus of Nazareth in founding the breakaway sect which later became Christianity, they brought this concept with them.

In contrast to the Christian concept of the Devil, Orthodox Judaism envisages the mythical figure of Satan as the tempter, a fallen angel who appeals to our vanity, passions and desires but who ultimately has no power over the soul, which remains pure regardless of how much we abuse our bodies, our emotions and our minds.

Kabbalah, being the esoteric core of Judaism, strips away the mythology entirely. It makes the figure of Satan the personal projection of each individual's inner nature, their shadow self rather than a separate character. Whenever we indulge our desires to excess against our better judgement, we are effectively invoking, or empowering, an unbalanced aspect of our personality against the 'angel' of our own conscience.

'God wanted to perfect His works by making a creature which was half divine and half earthly; this is Man whose body is coarse and earthly, while his soul is spiritual and heavenly. He set the earth and all its creatures below Man and gave him the means of drawing close to the angels who are there, some of them to control the movement of the stars and others to live in the elements. You can therefore recognise many of them by their signs or their characters and make them familiar and compliant.' – anonymous 12th-century author of *The Little Key of Solomon*.

## EXERCISE: ANGELS OF THE SEPHIROTH

To experience the energies and meet the angels associated with different sephiroth, simply insert the appropriate colour, angelic name and Divine name which correspond to the sephiroth from the following table. (Malkhut is used in this example.) Strictly speaking, the Divine names belong to the higher World of Emanation, Azilut, and only overlap the angelic world of Beriah at the heart centre (Tiferet) of Azilut. For practical purposes these have been superimposed on the angelic world to give a sacred name to each sephirah. Using the Divine names is far more effective than simply using a generic title such as God.

| Sephiroth | Colour | Divine name | Angelic name |
|---|---|---|---|
| Keter | Gold | *Ehyeh* (Eh-huh-yeh) | Metatron |
| Binah | White | *Elohim* (El-o-heem) | Zaphkiel |
| Hokhmah | White | *Jehovah* (Jeh-hoe-vah) | Raziel |
| Daat | Blue | – | – |
| Gevurah | Violet | *Yah* (Yar) | Samael |
| Hesed | Purple | *El* (El) | Zadkiel |
| Tiferet | Green | *Jehovah Elohim* (Jeh-hoe-vah El-o-heem) | Michael |
| Hod | Yellow | *Elohim Zevaot* (El-o-heem Zev-ah-oat) | Raphael |
| Nezah | Orange | *Jehovah Zevaot* (Jeh-hoe-vah Zev-ah-oat) | Uriel/Haniel |
| Yesod | Red | *El Hai Shaddai* (El High Shad-I) | Gabriel |
| Malkhut | Citrine, Olive, Russet, Black | *Adonai Ha Aretz* (Ado-nigh Ha Erets) | Sandalphon |

☆ Make yourself comfortable, close your eyes and begin by focusing on your breath. Take slow, deep regular breaths. With each exhalation feel the tension dissolve and drain out of your body through your fingertips and feet. With each inhalation visualise yourself drawing in a warm, calming light which revitalises every cell of your being.

☆ Now visualise yourself standing on the same vast mountain plateau that you had climbed to in your ascent of the World of Emanation. The temple of Malkhut is once again before you with its two formidable pillars of black onyx and white ivory.

☆ You enter its sacred space to stand before the altar, which is draped in a cloth whose colour corresponds to the quality of energy of Malkhut, the sephirah you will explore in this meditation. You should see either olive green, russet brown, citrine or black, for these are the colours of Malkhut, the Kingdom, the earth. If you see another colour, accept it for now, knowing that its significance will be revealed on your return.

☆ On the altar you find a menorah, the seven-armed candlestick symbolic of the sephiroth and the Four Worlds of Divine manifestation. It has been fashioned from a single piece of pure gold to represent the unity of all existence. You light the first of the candles and ask for the blessing of the Most High on the ritual that you are about to perform.

☆ Now intone the Divine name corresponding to this level aloud or to yourself. It is Adonai Ha Aretz, Lord of the Earth and the Visible Universe. Sound it slowly and with the conviction that you are invoking a specific aspect of God which is symbolised by this sephirah. Feel the sound of this most sacred name reverberating inside you and enveloping you. Repeat it several times until you can imagine it echoing to the edge of existence.

☆ Now intone the name of the angel corresponding with the sephirah of Malkhut. It is Sandalphon. As you repeat the angelic name a mist begins to form about the altar. From within a light begins to glow and pulsate, growing in intensity with each repetition of the name.

☆ Become aware of an angelic presence emerging from the light. Lower your eyes to shield them from the luminous brilliance of its being. Sense its angelic wings enfolding you. Open yourself to the infinite love of its embrace.

☆ Speak with it. Ask any questions that come to mind and listen attentively as it tells you how you can open more effectively to the angelic energy at this level on the Tree.

☆ Offer thanks when it indicates that the contact has come to a close. Ask that its blessing be with you until the next time you meet. Sense its presence fading as it returns to the light.

☆ When the presence has departed from this place and the light has faded, return your attention to your surroundings, the chair you are sitting in and focus once more on your breath. When you are ready, open your eyes and stamp your feet to ground yourself in Malkhut.

## EXERCISE: INVOKING THE ARCHANGELS FOR PROTECTION AND GUIDANCE

This guided visualisation is a traditional Kabbalistic method of invoking Divine power for protection. It uses the image of the four archangels, who are considered to be at the highest level of the angelic realm. You can think of them as personifying four divine attributes in the purest form.

☆ Make yourself comfortable and focus on your breath. When you feel sufficiently relaxed begin by visualising a tiny speck of brilliant white light manifesting in the centre of your forehead, at the third eye. See it growing larger and becoming brighter until it glows like a small sun before you. You can sense its brightness with your eyes closed. Despite its intensity, it is calming. So calming, in fact, that you want to absorb it. You are soon surrounded and wholly absorbed in Divine light, protected from head to toe within a huge bubble of light energy.

☆ When you are ready, invite the archangels to join you. You can say a prayer of your own choosing silently to yourself if you wish or repeat the following invocation: '*Almighty and loving father, hear my prayer. I ask for permission to call upon thy servants of light, the four archangels Raphael, Gabriel, Michael and Uriel, that I might be blessed with those aspects of thy Divine presence which they represent for the purpose of healing, protection and guidance.*

*If it is thy will, let it be so.'*
*'In the name of the almighty, blessed be He, the one God*
*EhYeh Asher Ehyeh\* who created Heaven and Earth, I summon*
*His servants of the light. Come to me in His name and with*
*His blessing or do not come at all.'*
**'Before me Raphael; behind me Gabriel, by my**
**right hand Michael; by my left hand Uriel.'**

☆ Now focus your awareness before you, where stands
the archangel Raphael. Repeat silently to yourself the
God name by which we test for deception at his level of
vibration: *Elohim Zevaot*. Sense the presence of Raphael
and the quality of his particular energy. How do you
envisage him? He may be attired in robes of his primary
colour, which is yellow, the colour corresponding to the
quality of energy in the solar plexus, the seat of the
emotions. From Raphael you can ask for the release of
emotional blockages, the strength to let go of deep-
rooted attachments and the healing of emotional wounds.
Raphael is the archangel personifying the Divine attribute
of Hod (Reverberation) on the Tree of Life.

☆ Now extend your awareness behind you. Sense the
presence of Gabriel. Repeat silently to yourself the God
name by which we test for deception at his level of
vibration: *El Hai Shaddai*. Gabriel personifies the Divine
attribute of Yesod (Foundation) on the Tree of Life,
corresponding roughly to the Base or Root chakra,
therefore you might envisage him robed in red. He will
revitalise you and give you strength if your vital energies are depleted.

\*'I am that I am'.

☆ Now focus on your right side where stands the archangel Michael, the Great Protector. Repeat silently to yourself the God name by which we test for deception at his level of vibration: *Jehovah Elohim*. Michael personifies the Divine attribute of Tiferet (Beauty) on the Tree of Life, energy which corresponds with the Heart chakra. His colour is green, symbolising the regenerative power of nature and the boundary between the physical and spiritual realms.

☆ Now become aware of the presence of Uriel. Repeat silently to yourself the God name by which we test for deception at his level of vibration: *Jehovah Zevaot*. From Uriel you can acquire courage, conviction and strength of purpose, the active attributes of the emotional sephiroth. Uriel personifies the Divine attribute of Nezah (Eternity) on the Tree and his energy corresponds roughly to the Solar Plexus chakra. He may appear adorned in orange, which is a blend of yellow and red, indicating passion under control of the emotions.

☆ Take your time to commune with the archangels. Ask of them what you will and receive any gifts they may give you with grace and gratitude. Do not be afraid to question the significance of their gifts or the symbols they bear.

☆ When you are ready, close the meditation with this invocation or one of your own choosing: '*I thank you servants of the light for the blessing of your presence and for your guidance and protection now, in the past and in the future. I ask that I may commune with you again but now I return you to the light. Shema Yisrael Adonai Elohanu Adonai Echad.*'*

*'Hear O Israel the Lord is our God, the Lord is One.'

☆ Once again become aware of your breathing, your body, the chair you are sitting on and your surroundings. When you are ready open your eyes.

# 6

# Ways of the Kabbalah

'The interpretation of the Qabalah is not to be found, however, among the Rabbis of the Outer Israel, who are Hebrews after the flesh, but among those who are the Chosen People after the spirit – in other words, the initiates.' – Dion Fortune

Non-Jews or those people unfamiliar with the Kabbalah can benefit and relate to it if they take it in the right spirit, as indicated in the above quote. This emphasises the universal nature of the teaching.

In Kabbalah there is no distinction between sacred and secular life. Just as everything in the universe is an expression of the Divine, so every action, feeling and thought of the Kabbalist is considered to be an expression of his or her conscious awareness of the God within and without. The three methods of achieving and sustaining this heightened state are action, devotion and contemplation, which are ways of engaging and focusing the physical body, the emotional body and the intellect.

**Action**   can take the form of a daily ritual. The word ritual has certain connotations for us today, but it does not have to be a traditional religious rite or an elaborate pseudomagical ceremony involving mystical signs and archaic incantations. The one crucial element of an effective Kabbalistic ritual is that it is a sincere act of worship, dedicated to the Divine.

**Devotion**   is traditionally considered to find expression in prayer, but it can be any selfless conduct that comes from the heart, such as caring for someone who is sick or infirm. That is why people who serve others with a grudging resentment are not carrying out a mitzvah ('good deed') but what Christians would consider a sin, for it is not the deed but the spirit of the deed that is encapsulated in devotion. The crucial element of devotion is a love of God and of all that God created. Counting one's blessings is a simple and effective form of devotion, resulting in a sense of gratitude and humility.

**Contemplation**   is the third way of Kabbalah. It involves reflection on spiritual matters such as the nature of God, the present state of the world, the hidden meanings behind sacred texts or speculating on the significance of an individual's life.

All three approaches are to be taken by the Kabbalist in the service of God and according to His will, but in so doing the individual is becoming more self-aware and evolving according to the Divine plan. When the three paths are traversed without ambition, spiritual pride or self-interest it invariably leads to the development of psychic powers, greater intuition and insight. It will ultimately lead to direct contact with the Divine.

## Contacting the Higher Self

There are many ways to establish a line of communication with the Adam of Azilut, or the Higher Self, as it is called in the Western esoteric tradition. All involve temporarily suspending awareness of the individual sense of self and the restless, ever demanding ego. In contacting the Higher Self you seek to realise your ultimate potential, to be a fully realised human being and to manifest the Divine on earth. The following exercise is designed to do this safely, but be prepared to redefine your sense of self! Most people will find it revealing, but some could find it unsettling. A few who make the connection and find themselves inspired to practise what is called automatic writing make the mistake of believing that they are communicating with an external intelligence (be it extraterrestrials, discarnate spirits or angels), because they are desperate for sensation rather than self-awareness. To avoid being seduced by your own ego, imagination or fears, ensure you are adequately grounded before attempting such an exercise. Reassure yourself through repeating an affirmation or prayer that you are going to contact your Divine self for your highest good and for no other purpose.

### EXERCISE: CONTACTING YOUR HIGHER SELF

☆ Begin by closing your eyes and focusing on your breath. Still the mind and raise your level of awareness by performing the grounding exercise, or utter a prayer of your own choosing to create a sacred space around you.

☆ When you feel relaxed, choose one affirmation from the selection listed below according to whatever theme is occupying your mind at the moment or has been causing you problems in the past. Write your chosen sentence once, then close your eyes and open yourself to the first thoughts that come into your mind. Give yourself approximately two minutes' silence in which to write down whatever comes into your mind, regardless of whether or not it makes sense to you at the moment.

☆ If nothing comes through, write 'nothing'. If you find yourself writing furiously before you have time to consciously think what it is that you are writing, as if you are taking dictation, then keep writing until the contact is ended by the Higher Self. Do not be nervous about asking appropriate questions. You are communicating with your own unconscious, which exists at a higher level of awareness than your conscious mind, so it is neither 'cheating' nor dabbling in the occult to ask the greater part of yourself what you already know but are simply not conscious of knowing.

☆ When the two minutes have passed write the affirmation a second time and listen for your inner voice once again. Do this 22 times in total.

☆ Repeat the exercise once each day for 11 days. Resist the temptation to analyse whatever comes through until you have completed each exercise, but when you do reflect on what you have written and pay particular attention to the use of 'I' and 'you', which should give a sense of this illusion of separation. And, as with all meditation exercises, do not try too hard or become frustrated if nothing comes through at first. It will if you persevere and cultivate a receptive attitude.

☆ The exercise should take about 45 minutes each time. Leave a gap of 11 days before choosing another sentence that you feel you need to work with. Do not be tempted to stop after just one or two sentences, as you will probably need to work through a complete cycle of affirmation before you are made aware of all the blocks that you need to clear in this lifetime.

## AFFIRMATIONS

*I am in my power. I am well and have abundant energy.*
*I am fulfilling my life purpose and have great joy and happiness.*
*I am perfectly acceptable as I am.*
*Money flows to me in a positive and abundant way right now.*
*I have the courage to achieve all that I desire.*
*I have perfect relationships always.*

# The Mystical Experience

The insights you receive through the exercise 'Contacting Your Higher Self' come through Daat, the unmanifest sephirah, often described as a veil or 'the abyss' by those who wish to romanticise the mysteries. These profound insights involve a mystical experience in which the individual catches a glimpse of the greater reality of which we are all an indispensable part, as for example, in Ezekiel's vision or Jacob's dream. From that moment on the visionary 'knows' the meaning of being at one with the universe, but often they find that language is inadequate to describe the quality of their experience.

Such experiences invariably change forever the life of the individual who takes the first step to 'become' the Divine being they have the potential to become, whether we call this the Higher Self or Adam Kadmon. From that moment of contact, however fleeting it may be, we are then in the world but not of it, to borrow a Buddhist expression.

Unfortunately, mystical experiences do not always guarantee lasting enlightenment, as the profusion of false prophets and mad messiahs throughout history will prove! The ego, or conscious mind, at the lower level of Yesod, can distort that reflection of the Higher Self, or the will can warp it. This distortion is a form of self-deception which has been practised through the centuries by self-righteous religious fanatics who have built cults or crusades on a single flash of insight. It is imperative not to force such visions upon an unbalanced psyche through drugs and spurious pseudo-spiritual practices, but instead to prepare oneself through steady practice. Adherence to a sound system, such as Kabbalah, which offers a firm foundation for increasing awareness prepares the mind for such a moment.

## The Halls of Heaven

These are the levels of increasingly refined consciousness which an enlightened person can attain. The higher Halls should be seen as seven levels of Heaven and not in finite human terms. The seven lower Halls are stages of psychological initiation.

The importance of establishing a firm foundation in all forms of spiritual work is stressed in the story of Rabbi Akiba, whose ascent through the seven Halls of Heaven is described in the Talmud. Legend has it that Rabbi Akiba, a renowned Merkabah teacher in 1st-century Palestine, attempted his ascent in the company of three other rabbis. However only Akiba's account survives, for the other three, it seems, were fatally unprepared. One died, another lost his sanity and the third was so shaken that he lost his faith.

Rabbi Akiba described his experience in the form of an allegory, but we can assume that in 'going down in the chariot', as it was then called, Akiba was effectively descending into the essence of his own being through the seven lesser Halls of the psyche, and then travelling in his astral body up through the seven higher Halls in the World of Creation, which correspond to seven stages on the central column of the Tree of Beriah (including the central triads).

The First of the higher Halls is the point at which the three lower worlds converge, namely the crown of the physical world, the heart centre of the astral world and the root of the world of essence. Here, in the Palace of the Curtain as Akiba calls it, lies the veil between the natural and the supernatural worlds, which can be drawn back to allow men to converse with the angels. The keys to entering this First Hall are conscious intent and devotion.

The Second Hall corresponds to the Yesod of Beriah. It is the province of the archangel Gabriel, who oversees the first stage in the return of souls to Paradise. The key to this Second Hall is purity.

The Third Hall exists at the first triad of the Tree of Beriah, formed by Hod, Yesod and Nezah. It is known as the Palace of Light and Fire. At this level the aspirant has passed beyond self-interest to the state of self-awareness under the influence of the sephiroth of Wisdom, Knowledge and Understanding. With self-awareness comes illumination of the hidden truths behind the sacred texts at the discretion of the archangels of Revelation and Tradition. The Hebrew word for this form of illumination is 'manna', from which the phrase 'manna from heaven' is derived. The key to this Third Hall is sincerity.

The Fourth Hall, guarded by the archangel Michael, is envisaged as the dimension of the Heavenly Jerusalem, the place at which the human and Divine worlds meet. Here Rabbi Akiba came into the Presence of the Lord, which can be understood as meaning that he rose to a level of consciousness equivalent to the lowest point of the Divine World of Emanation, Azilut. Here, tradition tells us, dwell the ten great spirits who constitute the Heavenly Assembly of Israel (namely, humanity) who watch over the progress of humanity under the guidance of the Messiah. This is the place of the fully-realised human being and therefore the key is self-realisation.

The Fifth Hall leads out of the fourth, just as a door in our dimension is both an entrance and an exit depending on perspective. Because of this, Michael is able to be both the guardian of the Fourth Hall and also one of the three archangels who preside over the Fifth, the other two being Samael and Zadkiel. Their presence corresponds to the three sephiroth of Severity, Truth and Love on the Tree of Beriah, and they must be balanced to attain psychological unity and a state of spiritual integrity. When Rabbi Akiba and the other mystics such as Ezekiel achieved this elevated state they were able to perceive the workings of Providence. The key to this Hall is holiness.

The Sixth Heaven is the Palace of the Will, where the Ruah Hakodesh, the Holy Spirit, resides. This is the level of Divine manifestation at which the intention of God to create was implemented. For Akiba and those who have broken free of the wheel of life, death and rebirth, it is the state where one loses the sense of individuality, uniqueness and the false sense of separation from the source. There is no key because entry to this Hall is by the Grace of Providence where one reunites with the Holy Spirit.

Finally, Akiba reached the Seventh Heaven, the realm symbolised by the Throne of Ezekiel's vision. Passing between the archangels Zaphkiel and Raziel, who personify the twin sephiroth of Binah (Understanding) and Hokhmah (Wisdom), at this level of consciousness he stood erect 'holding his balance with all his might' before the archangel Metatron. In the language of our own time this means that he attained this heightened state of detachment and perception through the unification of his physical, psychological and spiritual bodies. This is the Kabbalistic equivalent of the ecstatic state of enlightenment described in other traditions, but it is different. In Kabbalah enlightenment comes through a conscious ascent through the sephirotic trees of each of the upper and inner worlds, in a distinct and disciplined progression at the will of the Kabbalist.

We all ultimately rise in consciousness to self-realisation through the same process, but we usually do so through painful experiences over many lifetimes or through other paths using the same principles under different names (for example, my references to the chakras). In contrast, Kabbalah offers a gradual system of self-development and awareness so that we can attain this state while fully conscious.

We all travel to the same destination but by different paths. Without a unified system with which to orientate ourselves, such as the Kabbalah, we may take longer and be unable to assimilate the experiences to our advantage because we would be unaware of the specific stages involved.

## The Mystical Vision

Visions of the celestial scheme are not confined to Biblical prophets or even practising Kabbalists. Anyone can experience these insights and be transformed by the wonder of them at any time in their lives, regardless of their religious beliefs. They invariably occur after a period of intense searching for the meaning and purpose of life, as the playwright and author J. B. Priestley discovered.

Priestley's vision took the form of a lucid dream in which he was fully conscious of what he saw, yet was technically asleep. Kabbalists would describe this experience as being out of the body in which the visionary sees 'with the eyes of the spirit'. It is the same state that Jacob attained when he dreamed of the ladder ascending to heaven.

In this semi-dream state, Priestley found himself looking down from a high tower beneath which a vast flock of birds were migrating. As Priestley looked on, time appeared to accelerate as if he was part of a movie that had been mysteriously sped up. In front of his eyes generations of birds of every known species grew frail and died, to be replaced in the great aerial stream by newborn fledglings who also grew older and died within what seemed like seconds. Priestley was overcome with sadness to see each life pass by without apparent purpose. At this point he thought that it might be better if all living creatures, including ourselves, could be spared this apparently futile struggle. As if in answer to this thought, time moved up another gear causing the birds to rush past in a blur, and within this vast carpet of feathers he noticed a white flame leaping from body to body. He understood this to be the flame of life itself. 'What I had thought was tragedy,' he later wrote, 'was mere emptiness or a shadow show ... I have never felt before such deep happiness as I knew at the time of my dream of the tower and the birds.'

Priestley's vision is not specifically Kabbalistic in character or symbolism, but it confirms a central Kabbalistic principle which is that the impulse of evolution flows inexorably in accordance with the Divine will. And it will carry us with it if we do not attempt to impose our will upon it.

# 7

# Secrets of the Scriptures

'The Kabbalah opens up access to the occult, to the
mysteries. It enables us to read sealed epistles and books
and likewise the inner nature of man.' – Paracelsus.

## Esoteric and Exoteric

In many of the major religions there is both an exoteric (outer)
and an esoteric (inner) tradition. In Judaism the rituals,
customs and festivals are the exoteric expression of the
esoteric teachings on which the faith was founded, but of
which the majority of the community are unaware. Only those
familiar with Kabbalistic principles would know that even the
design of the synagogue is symbolic of the structure of existence, specifically the Four Worlds and the configuration of
the sephiroth, as are the vestments of the rabbis and the ritual
objects used in worship.

The seven-armed candlestick known as the Menorah has a
second function to its use in ritual and that is as an object for
contemplation. It is invariably made of one piece of metal to

symbolise the unity of the Divine World of Emanation. Its central column corresponds to the Pillar of Equilibrium and the outer arms to left and right correspond to the Pillars of Mercy and Severity. It features ten sephirotic positions plus one representing Daat, the unmanifest, and 22 decorations corresponding to the paths on the Tree of Life.

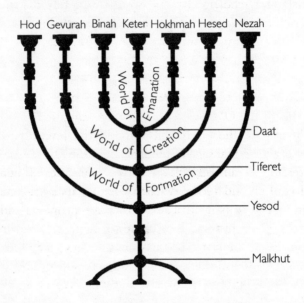

The Menorah and the Four Worlds

Even the vestments of the Rabbi or High Priest have a symbolic significance of which few members of a modern congregation would be aware. Over the physical form, which represents Malkhut, the Rabbi wears an undershirt representing the soul in the world of Yezirah. Over this he wears a blue surcoat to symbolise the celestial realm of Beriah and over this he has a gold coloured garment symbolising the Divine essence in the World of Azilut.

If a religion is to continue to have validity for succeeding generations, then it has to reconcile the two strands of its tradition, which could be seen as the substance and the reflection. If only the esoteric is emphasised, without regard to its practical application, the movement will cease to address the community at large and become a clique of occultists and scholars. It may even completely degenerate into a fundamentalist cult. If, however, only lip service is paid to the customs and rituals, out of a sense of duty, without understanding their purpose or meaning, then it will become increasingly irrelevant and will inevitably decline.

Kabbalah aims to reveal the hidden teachings encoded in the myths of the Old Testament for the enlightenment of all and not just for those who subscribe to the Jewish faith. In recounting the tribal saga of the Israelites, the Old Testament is addressing all humankind, for 'Israel' translates as 'humanity'. It is of secondary importance whether its stories have a basis in fact. Nor is it critical whether the prophets and the patriarchs were historical or fictional figures. Its primary purpose is to indicate – through allegory, parable and symbolism – the ultimate journey of each and every human being through the trials of life and beyond, back to the Divine.

## Exodus

In Exodus, for example, we are introduced to the 12 sons of Israel, who in the esoteric tradition symbolise the 12 basic human archetypes, whose characteristics are personified in the signs of the zodiac.

The descent of the Israelites into Egypt and their growth as a community can be seen as mirroring the stages in the life cycle of the individual (as described in Chapter 4), while their subsequent enslavement is considered to be a veiled reference to the confinement of the soul in physical form.

The rainbow-like aura that surrounds the body is symbolised in Joseph's coat of many colours, while Egypt represents the bondage of incarnation in the kingdom of Malkhut, our physical world, just as Babylon later became synonymous with any place of decadence. It is not a coincidence that the Hebrew word for Egypt translates as 'confined'.

It may also be significant that alchemy, a process which was symbolic of turning the base element of matter into the gold of pure spirit, takes its name from the Arabic phrase '*al chem*', meaning 'the art of Egypt'.

A rabbinical commentary on Exodus elaborates on the concept of incarnation, a subject which is not addressed in the Orthodox tradition. It states: 'As soon as Joseph died, the eyes of the Israelites were also closed as well as their hearts. And they began to feel the domination of the stranger.' This is a reference to the belief that our conscious connection with the upper worlds is severed at the age of five, when a veil is drawn across the third eye so that we are forced to concentrate on the physical life.

Joseph, the 'dreamer of dreams', is a symbol of childhood innocence. His death marks the onset of youth, with its emphasis on education and self-discipline, as the Israelites are subjected to the rigours of forced labour under Pharaoh.

The Exodus from Egypt would therefore be symbolic of the journey which all enslaved souls must make if they are to enter the land of milk and honey, the Promised Land of spirit. To reach our ultimate destination we first have to subjugate our lower nature and liberate our Higher Self, a process mythologised in Moses's killing of the Egyptian overseer. The 'official' written version of the incident in the Bible gives the impression that it was a straightforward murder, an impulsive act in which Moses took revenge on a sadistic over-seer for torturing a helpless Hebrew slave. The oral tradition, as written in the Talmud, gives a fuller account, with Moses murdering the man by invoking the Name of God. Clearly this is no simple killing, but a metaphor for calling on Providence to aid in a personal transformation.

After we pass through this same 'rite of passage' in our own lives it is frequently followed by a period of soul-searching, when we question our own values and those of society. This usually involves joining various esoteric, religious or philosophical groups, against whom we test the validity of our new ideas. In the Bible this stage is commonly illustrated by the prophets' sojourns in the desert, where they commune with their higher nature, often represented by God.

## Initiation and Revelation

In the story of Moses' spiritual awakening he was fortunate to find a teacher, Jethro, a priest of Midian, who would be his future father-in-law (a title which reveals further meaning), but first he had to draw a sapphire rod from the ground to prove his readiness for responsibility. Such initiation rituals are a common theme of quest literature, from the Norse sagas to the legends of King Arthur. They all serve a similar purpose. In the rabbinical commentaries and folklore of Judaism the sapphire rod is described as being a splinter from the Tree of Knowledge, engraved with ten holy letters which we can assume symbolise the sephiroth.

Having proven his worthiness and won the hand of Jethro's daughter Zipporah, Moses was then entrusted with tending the priest's flock of sheep. In the Bible a shepherd is often used as a metaphor for a teacher, an image enforced by the fact that Moses was initially given the youngest sheep to tend, then the older flock and finally the mature animals. In tending the flocks Moses, the tutor, also learned to control his own animal impulses and instincts rather than be driven by them, a fundamental stage in the ongoing process of self-discipline and self-awareness.

After accepting this role, the prophet was rewarded with a vision of an angel amid the flames of a burning bush, a phenomenon which equates with that moment of sublime insight which everyone is said to experience once in their lives, whether they seek it or not. In that moment our consciousness shifts from the physical plane through all four worlds simultaneously as we perceive the unity of existence and the presence of the Divine in each and every aspect. A clue to the esoteric meaning of this episode is to be found in the phrase 'the place on where thou standest is holy ground'. No place on earth can truly be said to be more holy than any other if the universe in totality is a reflection of the Divine. Instead the phrase echoes the experience of many mystics and visionaries, who describe having had a real sense of other-worldliness at such a moment, as if they had walked on sacred ground.

With this glimpse of a greater reality comes the choice to pursue the spiritual path or return to the mundanity of the material world. According to the Old Testament, Moses was no different from the rest of us in that he sought to assert his own will against the will of God, which was the voice of his own Higher Self. He initially refused to return to Egypt, which can be seen as the pursuit of self-interest. However, after some more soul-searching he saw the wisdom of returning to liberate his own people, who were in bondage. This act corresponds to initiating others into the tradition.

The stage was then set for what is perhaps the most gruelling test of all. Moses, as the evolving conscience, had

to persuade Pharaoh, who represents the senses, to relinquish control of the imprisoned Israelites, who symbolise the
unruly elements of the immature psyche.

## The Ten Plagues

This eternal struggle, which we all come to in our own time,
reaches a climax in the Old Testament with the account of
the ten plagues. These afflictions were not a supernatural
curse inflicted on the Egyptians by a partisan God, as the
Orthodox tradition would have it. A loving Father, heavenly
or otherwise, does not impose suffering on his own children,
no matter how unjust and cruel they may behave towards
each other. Injustice, as we would perceive it, is instead
addressed by the natural expansion and contraction of the
active and passive aspects of the Tree, aided by the laws of
karma. Contrary to popular belief, karma is not alien to the
Judaeo-Christian tradition. It is a central Kabbalistic concept
which was succinctly expressed by one of its most celebrated
exponents in the phrase, 'As you sow, so shall ye reap'. The
plagues can be seen instead as an excess of the forces symbolised in the sephirotic attributes resulting in imbalance in the
physical world – just as rain in moderation is welcomed to
help crops grow but an excess can cause flooding and
destruction. The plagues were orchestrated by Moses and
Aaron in four stages, with the former dealing with those
concerned with fire and air (hail, locusts and darkness) and
his brother implementing those corresponding to earth and
water (blood, frogs and lice) in a perversion of the unfolding
of the Four Worlds. Together they invoked the plague of
boils – an excess of contraction in contrast to hail which is an
excess of expansion (i.e. a bite as opposed to a blast).

Nature then took its course. The unhygienic conditions
created a plague of flies which affected the cattle, and then

the first-born of the Egyptians died from eating infected grain, as if cursed. (Ironically only the first-born were given grain as they were considered privileged by virtue of their status.)

## Crossing the Red Sea

Once the beleaguered Pharaoh had finally relented and allowed the slaves to go free the next critical episode in the Biblical story was the crossing of the Red Sea, which marks the Israelites', and thereby Everyman's, eventual commitment to the spiritual path. It symbolises the point of no return, when we take an irrevocable step away from the ephemeral attractions of the material world towards self-awareness and maturity.

The Exodus from Egypt can now be seen as a symbolic journey across the desert of life, where pleasures are as transient and insubstantial as a mirage and as artificial as the idols worshipped by the Hebrew masses in exile.

The image of the desert as a setting for the saga was not an arbitrary choice, nor one determined by the region in which it was written. It is as significant as the other elements in the Old Testament. The arid, lifeless landscape reminds us that in life we appear to be separated from the sustaining waters of the source from which we came, but that if we seek the Divine, even in this most inhospitable of places, guidance will be given, and we too shall enter the Promised Land.

# 8

# Kabbalah and
# the Tarot

'The Tarot, the most satisfactory of all the systems of
divination, rises from and finds its explanation in the Tree
and nowhere else ... when it is realised that the initiate
works the Tarot and the Tree together, and that they
dovetail into each other at every imaginable angle, it will
be seen that such an array of correspondences could be
neither arbitrary nor fortuitous.' – Dion Fortune

Two colourful legends are associated with the origin of the
tarot, the 78-card deck popularly but erroneously associated
exclusively with fortune-telling.

One stretches the credulity of even the most fanciful
esotericist by setting the scene on the lost continent of
Atlantis just prior to the cataclysm that legend says sent it to
the bottom of the ocean. According to this version the high
priests, philosophers and magicians of the ill-fated isle
designed the deck as a means of preserving their sacred
wisdom in symbolic form in the certainty that it would
survive as a game of fortune in the wider world, even if the

significance of the symbols were lost.

The other tale transfers the fateful meeting to Morocco where a select group of initiates sought to preserve the wisdom of the ancient world shortly before the destruction of the great library at Alexandria.

Neither tale is likely to be true, as the oldest surviving tarot cards date from the 15th century, and there is no evidence of any earlier versions. More significantly, the principles that the cards embody are indisputably Kabbalistic in a form that is peculiar to mediaeval Europe.

Four suits, most commonly called wands, swords, cups and pentacles, correspond to each of the four Worlds. Each suit comprises 14 cards, one for each sephiroth, plus a King, a Queen, a Knight and Page to denote the four sub-levels of Will, Creation, Formation and Action. In addition 22 trumps known as the Major Arcana relate to the 22 paths connecting the sephiroth on the Tree of Life and the stages of individual and cosmic evolution.

Eminent occultists outside the Kabbalistic tradition have struggled to assign the cards to various paths according to planetary correspondences and the symbolic meaning of the Hebrew alphabet. It is my belief that Eliphas Levi, A. E. Waite and the founding members of the Golden Dawn, to name but a few, allowed their enthusiasm for phenomena and archaic lore to obscure the simple and eternal truth that lay before their very eyes.

It is my understanding that the tarot was devised primarily as a Kabbalistic teaching tool, not as a navigational aid to the realms of spirit, nor as a means of divination. Although it is valid to use the picture cards as meditational gateways to specific areas of the astral plane equated with the paths on the Tree and to explore the psyche through their symbolism, I believe that the primary purpose of the cards was as a visual aid. The use of these symbols helped enforce the principles of the teaching on the unconscious mind of initiates. It would also have helped to introduce Kabbalistic concepts to a largely illiterate community outside of the tradition.

## The Tarot and the Tree of Life

In assigning the 22 cards of the Major Arcana to the paths on the Tree Levi, Waite, Crowley, Fortune and the other occult 'authorities' appear to have failed to consider a fundamental principle – that any set of correspondences must conform to both logic and natural laws, while reflecting the central theme of Kabbalah expressed in the ancient maxim 'As above, so below'.

If the tarot cards are to be placed on the Tree they must reflect the natural world, the life cycle of the individual and their increasing self-awareness in the ascent back up the Tree towards God. For that reason I have reassigned all the cards of the Major Arcana according to Kabbalistic principles, which I believe adds to an understanding of the Tree as an expression of these universal laws and also to each individual's progress through life (see page 112). I must emphasise once again that these descriptions and their positions on the Tree are entirely my own and do not equate with those of other initiates.

The colours that correspond to the sephiroth are reassigned according to the same principles on page 83, beginning with white for Keter and passing through the other primary colours in the natural sequence of the spectrum to the densest colour black for Malkhut. In this logical fashion all elements of the system are consistent and can be validated by the reader for themselves according to simple common sense and what they see reflected in the world around them.

The Tarot and the Tree of Life

The cards on the lower paths represent the forces at work in the physical world namely karma (the Wheel of Fortune) and free will and self-determination (the Fool) which seek balance in discernment (the World) which is the principal lesson of this life. On either side of the ego in the sphere of Yesod are the attendant vices of self-deception, indulgence, enslavement (the Devil) and false pride (the Tower).

The inner struggle between power in all its forms and love finds expression in the passions (the Lovers) at the Hod/Nezah axis, which is the lowest point of the emotional realm. On the vertical path between Yesod, the place of the ego and Tiferet, the place of the Higher Self, lies the Hanged Man who personifies self doubt and indecision. He is often pictured suspended by his heels from a tree, an appropriate image if you consider that in my scheme he is crucified, so to speak, on the cross of the passions between the persona and the Higher Self.

When we transcend or grow tired of indulging the senses and of playing the manipulative games of Hod, we go in search of something that will offer a meaning and purpose to life. This search is personified in the two cards which form the Hod–Nezah–Tiferet triad, namely the Hermit and the Star. The Hermit represents the search for self-awareness and the Star represents the guiding inner light that will lead to self-knowledge and awareness. Through the strengthening of this connection with the Higher Self we also attain a love of life (the Sun), which is complemented by an increasing inner awareness. This awakening invariably finds expression in the development of psychic and intuitive powers (the Moon). The Sun and the Moon also symbolise the qualities of inner reflection and worldly wisdom which come with maturity and experience.

Balancing the qualities that we simplify as Judgement and

Mercy is the card known as Temperance, more accurately described as restraint and moderation. On either side rising from the sphere of the Higher Self to the spheres of Wisdom and Understanding are the cards of the High Priest (or the Hierophant) and the Priestess. These equate with the acquisition of spiritual knowledge, faith in a positive outcome and strength of one's convictions, which lead to Wisdom and Understanding when balanced with experience of the world. These cards symbolise the inner growth of the individual.

I have placed the Death card between the Hierophant and the Priestess on the vertical path leading through Daat to indicate that there has to be an ending to the idea of a separate self if we are to cross the abyss of Daat to attain union with the Divine. In a personal reading this card will translate as the need for change to overcome an obstacle in order to reach a specific goal. It is a fallacy that the Death card is a negative 'omen'; neither, for that matter are the cards known as the Devil and the Tower. If these are drawn during a reading they should be regarded simply as self-defeating impulses which are there to be overcome on our inexorable path to fulfilment.

Once we have transcended our limitations and come to terms with our fears we cross the abyss into the realm of Adam Kadmon (the Magician), the fully realised human being who has command over the Four Worlds within himself and, thus, over his own life.

Completing the supernal triad are the Emperor and Empress, symbolising the fulfilment of the male and female principles within each of us. Beneath them on the outer pillars in order of descent are the cards of Judgement and Justice, which in the individual equate with compassion and a sense of responsibility.

It will be seen that the cards assigned to the outer paths reflect the structure of society with the Heads of State (symbolised by the Emperor and Empress) above the law of the land (Justice and Judgement), which is in turn enforced by soldiers and police (the Chariot and Strength), which are the outer expressions of order and civilisation. In the individual this is expressed in the quality of self-discipline.

## *Key to the Cards*

I have limited myself to a few key words when describing the significance of the other cards, for the reason that beginners can easily become bogged down in detail if they have to keep referring back to lengthy descriptions in a book. In doing so they lose the spontaneity essential when working with intuition. There is no need for a card in the sphere of Malkhut as this is the realm we occupy at present.

### *Wands*

This suit relates to ideas and aspirations – the spiritual aspect.

| | | |
|---|---|---|
| Ace | Keter | fulfilment; triumph through surrender to a Higher Will |
| II | Hokhmah | wisdom; success after a struggle; evaluation and appreciation |
| III | Binah | understanding; reasoned reflection and control over conflicting interests |
| IV | Daat | the blessings of Providence; unexpected good fortune; reconciling the needs of the spirit and the Will |
| V | Hesed | indecision, conflict and competition |
| VI | Gevurah | accomplishment; respite prior to renewed effort |

| VII | Tiferet | struggle for self-determination; identity crisis; confronting opposition |
| VIII | Nezah | trust to instinct in this matter to overcome unexpected obstacles |
| IX | Hod | learning through a difficult experience; temporary adversity |
| X | Yesod | wilfulness, obstinacy, or need for self-sacrifice, a burden or dilemma |

## Swords

This suit relates to our thoughts and intellect – the rational aspect.

| Ace | Keter | insight; realisation; peace of mind; self-acceptance |
| II | Hokhmah | intuition; self-reliance; reconciling and accepting ones strengths and weaknesses |
| III | Binah | melancholy; sentiment; a severing of emotionalties |
| IV | Daat | remembrance; time for reassessment of values and aims |
| V | Hesed | reason defeated by sentiment; forgiveness; acceptance of limitations and present circumstances |
| VI | Gevurah | responsibility; sense of obligation; desire to avoid confrontation |
| VII | Tiferet | indecision; evasion; self-deception |
| VIII | Nezah | loss of direction; self-defeating |
| IX | Hod | worry; irrational fears; coming to terms with loss |
| X | Yesod | end of illusions and ideals; need for stability and reassessment; finality |

## Cups

This suit relates to the emotions.

| Ace | Keter | ecstasy; happiness; unconditional love |
| II | Hokhmah | harmony; compromise; sharing |

| III | Binah | joy; friendship; the need to appreciate one's gifts and those of others; the need to be appreciated |
|---|---|---|
| IV | Daat | ingratitude and refusal to acknowledge the gifts of Providence; over reliance on luck |
| V | Hesed | acceptance of loss; need for courage to continue; preoccupation with the past |
| VI | Gevurah | magnanimity; obedience; the need to express emotion |
| VII | Tiferet | temptation; conflict between desire and the Higher Self; danger of self-delusion |
| VIII | Nezah | distinguishing between what is true and what is false; a search for meaning and real values |
| IX | Hod | self-satisfaction; the successful pursuit of self-interest; abundance |
| X | Yesod | fulfilment from a firm foundation and a focus for the affections |

## *Pentacles*

This suit relates to material progress.

| Ace | Keter | prosperity and new opportunities; dominion over one's personal world |
|---|---|---|
| II | Hokhmah | stability and security through flexibility |
| III | Binah | mastery of work, craft or career through greater understanding |
| IV | Daat | reward for devotion; the need for centring, balancing and grounding |
| V | Hesed | financial worries; pride; fear of failure |
| VI | Gevurah | responsibility for making sound judgements; need for generosity |
| VII | Tiferet | a productive period; reaping what has been sown and cutting out what is no longer productive |
| VIII | Nezah | a period of learning, acquiring new skills and experience |
| IX | Hod | a period of leisure, acquisition and achievement. |
| X | Yesod | a period for questioning perceptions and asserting one's independence; discernment. |

As previously stated the four court cards relate to the four elements within each world – fire, air, water and earth – but they can be roughly equated with the following human characteristics for the purposes of a reading.

King of Wands: strong will, enlightenment and imagination
Queen of Wands: empathic, understanding
Knight of Wands: far-sighted, shrewd judgement
Page of Wands: decisiveness, determination, tenacity

King of Swords: maturity, integrity, creative accomplishments
Queen of Swords: a person of principle, faithful, patient
Knight of Swords: prolific, impetuous, inspired
Page of Swords: curious, seeker, independent and self-sufficient

King of Cups: restraint; need for sensitivity and mediation; controlled emotions but a passionate nature
Queen of Cups: devoted, responsible, compassionate
Knight of Cups: love of life, idealistic and enthusiastic
Page of Cups: romantic, loyal, supportive, friendship

King of Pentacles: successful leader, dynamic personality, wordly wisdom and experience
Queen of Pentacles: prudent, productive, practical and protective
Knight of Pentacles: ambitious, energetic, reliable
Page of Pentacles: sensual nature, restless, hungry for success and recognition

## *Working With the Tarot*

The enduring appeal of tarot rests largely with the unerring accuracy of its insights into the psyche and potential future of those who consult the cards. And yet, even those who work with the tarot on a daily basis find it difficult to explain how it works. No one, to my knowledge, has been able to explain how a randomly shuffled deck can produce a selection of cards that time and again appear to have a significance for the person who has requested the reading. The standard answer is that the Higher Self selects the significant cards and places them in the necessary order in the blink of an eye while the shuffling is taking place. I find this too incredible to accept, yet I have studied tarot with an experienced and highly intuitive teacher and can vouch for the validity of the system from personal experience.

It is my conclusion that the selection of cards is indeed random and that no supernatural agency is involved in their selection, but that the readings are no less valid. No matter which cards are picked they will have some relevance for the client because they are based on universal archetypes symbolising the Divine attributes within all of us. But the reader must be a genuine 'sensitive' or psychic to have a chance of giving an accurate reading, which they would have given anyway. The cards serve merely as a focus and stimulus for innate psychic abilities, stilling the conscious mind and allowing the Higher Self to be heard.

For this reason anyone can use the cards to explore their own psyche, to develop greater self-awareness and to seek guidance to specific questions at crucial moments in their life. A simple but useful exercise for the beginner involves choosing one card from the Major Arcana and meditating upon it. Visualise yourself inside the picture asking the character in the card to explain the various symbols and reveal something of the path that they personify. There are two particular spreads that the beginner should find useful and revealing. The first is a spread for seeking spiritual guidance and the second spread, based on the pattern of the Tree of Life, can be used to explore the psyche.

### EXERCISE: SPREAD FOR SPIRITUAL GUIDANCE

☆ Shuffle all the cards thoroughly before you begin.

☆ Shuffle again while asking each of the questions listed below. After each question take the top card and place it face down in the order indicated.

☆ When you have all eight cards before you, turn them face up and trust your intuition to give an accurate interpretation. The traditional interpretations may not always be relevant to your current circumstances and cannot take account of your personality, so use them only as a general guide.

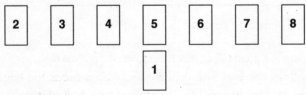

### Questions
1. What point have I reached in my spiritual growth, and what are my current concerns?
2. What are the recurring themes in my life?
3. What is the primary issue that needs to be resolved to fulful my life's purpose?

4. What do I need to understand more fully or look at from a new perspective?
5. What do I need to help me come to terms with any difficulties in my life?
6. What do I need to do now to make the most of the guidance I have been given?
7. What general guidance is offered for my future growth and well-being?
8. What is my ultimate potential in this life?

## A Sample Reading

During the writing of this book I did a reading for a lady who felt that she had lost her way in life and was eager to know what her particular path might be and how she could fulfill her true potential. I interpreted the cards that she drew as follows:

The presence of three cards from the suit of Swords suggested that this was a cerebral person with a strong academic interest, perhaps a teacher or student. The two cards from the suit of Cups indicated an emotional concern, while the single Pentacle showed that this was not linked to material gain.

**1) Four of Pentacles:** I interpreted this card as indicating that she had found fulfilment and a focus for her energy in her home life. Pentacles are linked to the home as well as to possessions, professions and wealth. It transpired that she had given up a promising academic career and part-time job as a college librarian to look after her three young children and though she enjoyed being a wife and mother she was feeling slightly resentful that she no longer had a life of her own.

**2) Five of Cups:** This card indicates that the subject is clinging to an emotional attachment which is preventing them from progressing or debilitating them by wasting their energy on regrets. After I had explained the meaning of this card the lady told me that her parents had divorced when she was still a child and that in her teens she had a bitter court battle with her father over an inheritance. Although her mother had remarried and the lady now had a family of her own she was still haunted by the feeling that her father had rejected her. She was also still finding it hard to forgive herself for having given up a university degree course to get married and start a family.

**3) The Magician:** This character is symbolic of Adam Kadmon, the fully realised human being who has come to terms with their limitations and fears and now exerts command over their own life. If this card is drawn in answer to question three it indicates that the person concerned is holding themselves back from fulfilling their potential. The most likely reason for this being that they believe that they are either unworthy of success or that they cannot believe that this potential lies within them. It transpired that the lady concerned believed that she had to be fully qualified and highly experienced to succeed at anything in life, except of course for motherhood. She had always been torn between her academic aspirations and her belief that she did not possess the intellectual capacity of her fellow students, although she would acknowledge that this was absurd.

**4) Nine of Swords:** This card in the context of the question told me that her irrational fears were undermining her potential and clouding both her self-image and her vision for the future. It also hinted at the possibility that she was so preoccupied with the possible outcomes of her actions, of imagined failure, that she was preventing herself from going out into the world and seeing what opportunities arose.

**5) Eight of Swords:** This card indicates that the subject can be their own worst enemy and that they should accept that their difficulties might be of their own making or possibly even a product of their own imagination. If instead they trust in their intuition and pursue their ambitions they might find that the imagined obstacles never materialise.

**6) Nine of Cups:** The card's answer to this question appears to be that she needs to acknowledge her right to self-determination now and again, leaving her husband in charge of the children even if it is only to play sport, join an adult education class or see friends once or twice a week.

**7) Strength:** This card suggested that she needed to be more self-disciplined and determined to see things through.

**8) Ten of Swords:** Her ultimate potential, according to this card, is to be free of illusions and unrealistic ideals, to see the world as it is and not as she would like it to be. And then to accept it as such.

## THE TREE OF LIFE SPREAD

☆ Before shuffling the cards, select the card that corresponds to your astrological sign and in the spread place it at Tiferet (position X), where it will stand in for your objective, Higher Self. The other cards will then be qualified by this central influence. Choose the card for position X from the following list:

| Birthdate | Astrological Sign | Tarot Card |
|---|---|---|
| 22 December–19 January | Capricorn | The Devil |
| 20 January–18 February | Aquarius | The Star |
| 19 February–20 March | Pisces | The Moon |
| 21 March–19 April | Aries | The Emperor |
| 20 April–20 May | Taurus | The Hierophant |
| 21 May–21 June | Gemini | The Lovers |
| 22 June–22 July | Cancer | The Chariot |
| 23 July–22 August | Leo | Strength |
| 23 August–22 September | Virgo | The Hermit |
| 23 September–23 October | Libra | Justice |
| 24 October–21 November | Scorpio | Death |
| 22 November–21 December | Sagittarius | Temperance |

☆ Next, enter into a meditative state by focusing on the breath and allowing the restless mind to settle into stillness. When you feel relaxed and open to higher influences shuffle the remaining cards thoroughly while asking the Higer Self for guidance.

☆ Take ten cards face down from the top of the deck. Place them on the Tree of Life in the order indicated.

☆ The cards can be read as follows:

**1. Malkhut:** relates to the questioner's present condition and attitude.
**2. Yesod:** represents the hidden hopes, fears and desires in the unconscious.
**3. Hod:** indicates the questioner's attitude to the world and their perception of it.
**4. Nezah:** relates to relationships and emotional needs.
**5. Gevurah:** indicates what is needed to motivate the

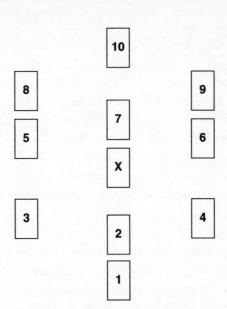

questioner into taking the next step.

**6. Hesed:** this card relates to a source of compassion and assistance, either from within oneself or from another person. It can indicate a source of outside help such as a friend, spiritual teacher or family member, whose support might be needed in making the next step in one's life.

**7. Daat:** this card indicates the forces that are currently, and possibly also continually, obstructing progress and personal development. These can be self-created obstacles generated by the unconscious mind to delay having to face what lies beyond the veil of Daat, such as a lack of self-discipline, or addiction to a negative relationship. There are innumerable ways in which we can hold ourselves back from further growth, such as the fear of responsibilities or even fear of success, all of which should be indicated and identified by the card at this position.

**8. Binah:** the passive female aspect of the psyche, concerned primarily with understanding. This card indicates the potential that can be attained through reason, intuition and experience.

**9. Hokhmah:** the active male aspect of the psyche, concerned primarily with wisdom. This card indicates the potential that can be attained through an assimilation of knowledge, revelation and experience.

**10. Keter:** relates to the ultimate aim or ambition.

☆ The cards should also be considered in relation to their respective triads with cards 7, 8, 9 and 10 corresponding to the intellect; X, 5 and 6 relating to emotional matters and 1, 2, 3 and 4 corresponding to the physical and worldly concerns.

## A SAMPLE READING

The following reading serves as a good example of what can be revealed by this spread. The subject was a teaching colleague who was interested in the spiritual path, but slightly nervous of what he might encounter if he joined a meditation group. I interpreted the cards that he drew as follows:

**1) Malkhut – The Star:** This card symbolises the inner guiding light and in this context indicates that the subject should follow their awakening intuition which is prompting them to seek further knowledge.

**2) Yesod – The Fool:** This card indicates a certain confidence to stride out into the unknown in search of self-determination, but also a fear that he might not be sufficiently prepared for what he imagines he might find there.

**3) Hod – Five of Swords:** The questioner's perception of the world appears to be clouded by sentiment. The card indicates that a less idealistic view might lead to fewer disappointments.

**4) Nezah – The Sun:** A very positive card which in this context is urging the subject to balance their intellectual pursuits with an uninhibited love of life, not to neglect the 'inner child' for the intellectual adult.

**5) Gevurah – The Hanged Man:** This card appears to suggest that the subject is either reluctant to relinquish his material possessions and earthly pleasures for the promise of spiritual development, or that his efforts to progress are undermined by self-doubt and indecision.

**6) Hesed – The Tower:** This card is traditionally seen as being negative, the destruction of all our carefully constructed plans. However, I interpret it as indicating a need to deconstruct our self-erected illusions, the high walls that we have erected around our true selves to keep the world at bay. The source of assistance referred to in the spread can now be seen as the inner voice which will guide us if we can only silence our restless minds and listen.

**7) Daat – Eight of Swords:** The main obstacle to my colleague's progress appears to be his own fears or feeling of unworthiness.

**8) Binah – Three of Pentacles:** According to this card my colleague's potential through a synthesis of reason and intuition is to become a master of his craft, i.e. a better teacher.

**9) Hokhmah – Ten of Pentacles:** According to this card greater knowledge and experience could bring him maturity and fulfilment through him becoming more self-contained and secure in his own beliefs.

**10) Keter – Strength:** His ultimate aim or ambition is inner strength and courage to face and overcome adversity.

# 9

# The Sacred Magic
# of Kabbalah

'Magic is the art of producing changes of consciousness in
accordance with the will.' – Dion Fortune.

There are many ways to experience the magic of Kabbalah
without having to make a lifetime study of the Torah texts
that are the foundation of the Old Testament or the Talmud
and its mass of rabbinical commentaries.

One of the most practical and effective methods available
to those outside of, or estranged from, the orthodox tradition is known as pathworking. The term 'pathworking' is
derived from Kabbalistic practice, but its origins as a meditation technique are believed to go back to the initiation rites
of the Summerians and the Chaldeans. The ancient Egyptians
developed the technique for the channelling of the wisdom
and teachings of their gods whom we could consider as being
discarnate spirits and the Higher Self.

Pathworking is a specific form of guided meditation in
which the practitioner travels the 22 paths connecting the
sephiroth on the Tree of Life through the imagination to

experience the energies which are unique to each. In traditional forms of guided meditation the practitioner is asked to close their eyes and imagine a particular type of landscape for the purposes of relaxation, or they may be asked to visualise a stressful situation so that they can work through an emotional problem. In both cases it is purely an imaginative exercise, although the results may be real enough.

But in pathworking we consciously activate the imagination to cross the borderland between the conscious and unconscious mind and then travel beyond into the world of spirit. Once we have cast ourselves adrift, so to speak, in these uncharted waters our only companions are the angelic guides assigned to each sephirah. Their appearance in the form of archetypal symbols confirms that we are strengthening our connection with the non-physical dimensions. These inhabitants of the inner and upper worlds have an independent existence quite distinct from the products of our imagination. With practise and experience it becomes easier to distinguish between insight and illusion, but for the beginner it is enough to know that if we can manipulate an image in meditation then we can dismiss it as a product of our imagination. However, if it appears spontaneously, if only for an instance, and has the quality of a vivid dream, then it is almost certainly of significance.

'In his ascent the mystic is irradiated by the light of the tree and in his descent the light finds a medium through which to flow back into the daily world [...]. In the descent a magic is worked and all the pretended way of ascent (through visualisation meditation) is rendered "greater than reality".' – Chaim Vital (1543–1620)

## Pathworking and the Psyche

Pathworking is a technique which has recently been enthusiastically adopted by many New Age self-help gurus for use in creative visualisation exercises, where the setting is freely adapted to suit the culture or personal interest of the individual. There are now pathworking exercises in the Grail legends, with King Arthur, Lancelot and Guinevere as key figures, in the Egyptian Mysteries, with Osiris, Seth and Isis in the corresponding roles, and even in the Norse Sagas for those with a penchant for the heroic quest. Some of these visualisations tend to indulge the adolescent fantasies of those who enjoy role-playing games, but in principle at least all are valid working methods for inner exploration because they invoke the same universal archetypes as those symbolised by the sephiroth.

Pathworking is now practised outside of esoteric circles in the field of Jungian psychotherapy where, known as 'active imagination', it is used to guide the patient into the realms of the unconscious. So, whether we attach magical or psychological labels to this technique we are effectively treading the same path for the same purpose – self-awareness and development. The distinction between the secular and the sacred methods is that in the latter the explorer has a fair idea of where they are going and what they are going to meet when they get there. In Kabbalah the initiate is even equipped with what is effectively a map of the inner world of the psyche and the upper worlds of the spirit.

The following exercises are the cornerstones of Kabbalistic practice. The first is designed to give access to the unique qualities of a specific sephirah and should ideally be done once a week for a month  before embarking on an exploration of another sphere.

The beginner is advised to start with an exploration of each of the sephiroth on the lower triad relating to the personality, before moving up to the three sephiroth of the middle triad, relating to the individual soul, the essence of our being. Finally, an ascent can be made into the three sephiroth of the supernal triad, representing the universal spirit.

In this example the choice of sephirah is Hod. To explore another sphere simply substitute the relevant sephirotic name together with the corresponding angelic and Divine names at the appropriate place.

## EXERCISE: TEMPLE OF THE SEPHIROTH

☆ Make yourself comfortable, close your eyes and relax. Then begin as usual by focusing on the breath.

☆ Visualise yourself entering a vast temple complex with corridors, cloisters and galleries connecting ten small private rooms or chapels for contemplation. In each sanctuary you will be welcomed by a guide who has been assigned to offer you guidance and healing of mind, body and spirit. They will answer any questions you may have of a spiritual or secular nature, but you need to ask them for help as they will not intervene in human affairs unless called upon to do so. These temple guides may appear in a variety of forms and may alter their appearance on subsequent visits, so you may wish to ask them to explain the significance of the form in which they appear.

☆ On this visit you are going to experience the energy of the temple of Hod and meet its guide, but as always we must begin by visiting the first temple, through which we gain access to the other levels. This is

Malkhut, whose floor is composed of black and white squares symbolising the interdependence of the two complementary universal forces.

☆ Imagine yourself seated on a large black comfortable chair carved out of a single slab of stone. Here you await the temple guide. Before you lies the altar, with its seven-armed golden candlestick, the menorah. Two candles have been lit as is customary to sanctify this sacred space and draw the guides into service. To the left and right of the altar are the two massive pillars symbolising the active male and the passive feminine attributes – one of black onyx, the other of white ivory.

☆ In the half-light of the candle flames you can discern three curtains against the far facing wall, behind which lie the doorways leading to the inner temples. On each of these curtains hangs a tapestry bearing the design of a tarot card. On the right-hand door is the tarot card of the Fool (symbolising self-determination and free will), in the centre is the card depicting the World (the entrance to the unconscious) and on the left door is the card known as the Wheel of Fortune, which often depicts the four Holy Creatures of the elements (the path of karma).

☆ It is now time to invoke the presence of the temple guide and ask for his or her assistance. You can use the following invocation, although it is more effective if you phrase this in your own words:

'My Lord Sandalphon (or appropriate name) I come into your presence in the name of Adonai Ha Aretz, the Lord of the

*Earth and the Visible Universe, that I might grow and evolve according to the Divine Will and for my Highest Good. I seek your assistance, guidance and protection while I am in this sacred space.'* Then add, *'I now ask your permission to exit through the left-hand door.'*

(Note: You may also choose to use the angelic name which corresponds with the sephirah rather than address the guide anonymously, see page 83.)

☆ The guide should then move across to the left-hand door and draw back the curtain, inviting you to climb a vast staircase to a building in the far distance. Feel your-self growing lighter with each step that you take towards the temple of your choice.

☆ Do not be tempted to stray off the path for any reason whatsoever, nor should you pay attention to any sounds or images to either side. Eventually you reach the entrance to the temple of Hod, which is flanked by two pillars of yellow sandstone.

☆ Knock upon the door and ask permission to enter. You can use the invocation above, substituting the appropriate Divine Name which is *Elohim Zevaot* and the angelic name *Raphael*.

☆ Find your seat in the temple before the altar, which is draped in a yellow cloth. Try to sense the quality of this sacred place. It is the temple of the mental processes. You should have a sense of the clarity of thought which is characteristic of this level, a clarity which is unclouded by emotional concerns.

☆ After a few moments you sense the presence of the temple guide. In what form does it appear? You may wish to ask the guide to reveal aspects of this sphere that have been concealed from your conscious mind, or simply request their blessing, which is a way of opening up to a greater awareness and understanding of this quality in your own psyche.

☆ When you are ready, thank the guide and ask if you may return another time. Then leave your seat, come out of the temple of Hod and return to the temple of Malkhut down the staircase and through the curtained doorway. Pass swiftly through and return to the daylight. Sense your surroundings and focus once again on your breath. Then open your eyes.

## EXERCISE: PATHWORKING

This exercise is designed to give an impression of the relationship and interplay between the energy patterns of the sephiroth and so develop a better balance between them. In this example the mental processes symbolised by Hod are to be balanced by the emotional forces of Nezah to achieve a clarity of thought which focuses on the positive aspects of the emotions but is unclouded by irrational feelings such as fears and sentiment.

☆ Begin by following the previous exercise from Malkhut to Hod as above. Instead of returning down the steps after visiting Hod, look across to the right and visualise the path, corridor, tunnel, cloister or gallery which connects the Temple of Hod to the Temple of Nezah. Imagine yourself inside the Tree of Life glyph if it helps.

☆ Travel this path to Nezah, the temple of the emotions while retaining the vivid impression of the mental clarity you gained at Hod, so that when you enter the temple of Nezah you sense the positive aspects of the emotional sphere, such as compassion, appreciation, love and joy, rather than the turmoil which they can bring when imbalanced. The path represents a state of consciousness which is the synthesis between these two qualities and is symbolised by the tarot card of the Lovers. If you are sensitive to this level at this time you may see an image associated with this card.

☆ When you reach the temple of Nezah, knock and ask permission to enter using the Divine name *Jehovah Zevaot* and the angelic name *Uriel*.

☆ As you sit before the altar, which is draped in an orange coloured cloth, and await the guide, you recall a time in your life when you felt so good that you felt compelled to express your happiness by giving a token of your affections to someone else. And as you recall that occasion and re-experience those feelings, know that you have control over these emotions at all times and that they do not have the power to overwhelm you.

☆ As always you may ask the temple guide when it appears to reveal the significance of this experience or to give you an insight into the nature of the emotions. Or you may simply ask for their blessing, which is a way of opening up to a greater awareness and understanding of this quality in your own psyche.

☆ When you are ready, thank the guide and ask if you may return. Then leave the temple and retrace your steps. By returning through Hod you will reinforce the importance of mental clarity, as it applies to balancing the emotions. When you find yourself outside the temple complex become aware of your surroundings and focus on your breath. Then open your eyes.

For reference, the magical images associated with each sephiroth are as follows:

| | |
|---|---|
| Malkhut | A young woman wearing a crown and seated upon a throne |
| Yesod | A naked muscular man |
| Hod | An androgynous figure |
| Nezah | A beautiful young woman |
| Tiferet | A young king or a child |
| Gevurah | A charioteer |
| Hesed | A mature king on his throne |
| Binah | An older woman |
| Hokhmah | A bearded figure |
| Keter | An elderly king |

Do not be concerned if you see imagery which does not match the listed archetypes. Each journey is unique to the individual, and may have a different resonance each time, depending on personal circumstances. If the significance of the image eludes explanation, consult a reputable dictionary of symbols. (I recommend *The Hutchinson Dictionary of Symbols* by Jack Tresidder and my own *Complete Book of Dreams* which includes a comprehensive dictionary of symbols.)

Although Kabbalah is simple in essence, beginners can easily become overwhelmed by the mass of detail and frustrated by the apparently contradictory correspondences which different mystery schools have attributed to the various sephiroth and the connecting paths. (Mystery schools are esoteric groups dedicated to preserving, practising and teaching what has been variously known through history as the Ageless Wisdom and the Perennial Philosophy. Their techniques and titles differ but their ultimate aim is the enlightenment of the individual and union with the Divine.) If this occurs, return to the spirit rather than the letter of the tradition with a visualisation such as the one outlined below. Open to your own intuition to reveal the truth of what you feel is being obscured or concealed from you. Know that your intuitive understanding is as valid as those who have trodden this path before you.

## EXERCISE: GROUNDING THE ENERGY

☆ Begin by closing your eyes and focusing on your breath. Take slow, deep regular breaths and sense the tension draining out through your feet with every exhalation. Draw in the light of relaxation with every inhalation. Become aware of it energising every cell of your being.

☆ Now visualise yourself standing on a mountain plateau with the dawn sky above you. It is that transient moment when the sun is rising, but the moon is still clearly visible. It is strangely calm and yet not too far off you can see storm clouds gathering. Already the atmosphere is charged with the energy of creation.

☆ You are on the site of what was once a sacred

temple. Two formidable pillars, one of black onyx and the other of white ivory, stand before you on either side of a stone altar. They are all that remains of the inner temple, but as you step up to the altar you can sense the energy within the stones is as potent as ever it was and it is now waiting to be released.

☆ On the altar you find a chalice, which is a symbol of female energy, and a small dagger, symbolising the male aspect. Taking up the chalice in your left hand you notice that it is filled with an aromatic mixture of water and incense. Taking the dagger in your right hand you discover that it has a short inscription on the hilt. What does it say?

☆ The storm clouds are now overhead and you sense that this is the moment you have been waiting for. Raise the dagger and intone the Divine name ('I Am That I Am').

☆ In an instant the dark clouds part and, from the light beyond them, a flash of lightning arcs through the sky and strikes the dagger, sending a bolt of Divine energy through you. It energises and balances the sephiroth on the living Tree within before grounding itself in the rock on which you stand. You are not harmed, but are more full of life than you have ever felt before at the spiritual, mental, emotional and physical levels simultaneously.

☆ Now plunge the still smouldering dagger into the chalice and watch as the water instantly turns to steam. You breathe the heady vapour of the incense and feel yourself expanding beyond your physical body.

☆ Visualise yourself growing heavenwards like a mighty oak tree branching outwards and upwards towards the sun and the moon, the source and sustenance of your being. Sense yourself drawing energy up from the earth where your feet are anchored as if they had set down roots. And draw it down from the heavens, where the warmth of the sun and the radiance of the moon bathe your body and soothe your spirit. Feel the fresh breeze on your face and the refreshing dew on your skin. Soak up as much of this vital energy as you feel that you need at this moment in your life.

☆ When you are ready to return simply draw back down into your body, become aware of your surroundings, the seat you are sitting on and finally the rhythm of your breathing. Then open your eyes.

'The magical is a great hidden wisdom … No conjuration, no rites are needful; circle-making and the scattering of incense are mere humbug and jugglery. The human spirit is so great a thing that no man can express it; eternal and unchangeable as God Himself is the mind of man; and could we rightly comprehend the mind of man, nothing would be impossible to us upon the earth.' – Paracelsus

## Closing Down

It is important to end each meditation session with a simple grounding, clearing and balancing exercise. One method is to simply visualise the sephiroth as they are imprinted within the body and count down from crown to base, stamping the feet to reconnect with the physical world. Another method is to perform the Kabbalistic cross.

The cross has been the single most enduring symbol of Christianity since the crucifixion, but it was a significant symbol for diverse cultures around the world thousands of years before the time of Jesus. For the ancient Chinese it represented the number ten, the symbol of totality, and also the heavenly ladder by which the soul was said to ascend to the celestial kingdom. It is possible that migrating mystics from the East introduced both of these ideas to the early Jewish mystics, for they are echoed in the imagery of Jacob's dream and in the number of the sephiroth.

While that is a matter for speculation, it is certainly true that the cross was a central symbol for the early Kabbalists in the centuries before Christ. It signified the Tree of Life in a condensed and instantly recognisable form, with the vertical line representing the ascensional impulse and the horizontal axis representing the earth plane. But, as with all potent symbols, it also had secondary significance, which the initiates would contemplate in their meditations. The four arms of the cross represented the four worlds, the four elements within each, the four cardinal points of the physical universe and later, the four archangels. That is why it was ultimately adopted as the Christian symbol in preference to the chi-rho monogram which had been the sect's original emblem.

As an initiate of the Nazarenes, Jesus would have been familiar with the occult significance of the cross, a fact he demonstrated when he incorporated both it and the kabbalistic principles which it symbolises into the words of the Lord's Prayer. Dion Fortune says: 'Where may we look more aptly for our occult inspiration than to the Tradition which gave us the Christ?'

You can use the following exercise to make a connection with the Christ consciousness or simply to balance and strengthen the sephiroth on the Tree within the psyche before and after each meditation. It should be performed while standing facing east.

## EXERCISE: THE KABBALISTIC CROSS

☆ Begin by focusing upon the breath. When you feel relaxed, visualise a ball of intense white light above your head. Draw it down through your body to cleanse and energise all four levels of your being. Sense its warmth pulsing within you as it passes through all the energy centres before draining out of the soles of your feet. You are now standing in a pool of living light, with your energy centres balanced and energised.

☆ Place your palms together as if in prayer, with finger-tips touching in representation of the unity of the ten sephiroth. Ask for the blessing of the Most High for the day or night ahead and specifically for its loving presence in the rite or meditation you are about to perform.

☆ Then, with the tips of the fingers of your right hand, touch the middle of your forehead between the brows corresponding to the place of the Third Eye and intone, silently or aloud, the Hebrew word *Ateh* (*'Thine is'*). Then draw down the light from this point, again with the tips of the fingers of the right hand, to the heart centre and intone *Malkhut* (*'The Kingdom'*).* Then touch the right shoulder and intone *Vegevurah* (*'And the power'*) and next the left shoulder and intone *Vegedulah* (*'And the Glory'*). Finally bring both palms together again as in prayer, with thumbs pointing upwards in the centre of the chest, and intone *Le Olam Oman* (*'Forever, amen'*).

*Although Malkhut corresponds to the feet, here for practical purposes the heart is used to denote the grounding centre.

# Glossary

**angel** A benign supernatural entity (from the Greek *angelos* meaning 'messenger')

**Asiyyah** The World of Action – our physical world

**Azilut** The World of Emanation

**Beriah** The World of Creation – the realm of the spirit

**Binah** Sephirah of Understanding or Reason

**chakra** Energy centre in the subtle body

**Daat** The unmanifest sephirah of Higher Knowledge

**esoteric** Hidden inner tradition/teachings

**exoteric** Outer tradition/teachings

**Four Worlds** The four realms in descent from the Divine

**Gevurah** Sephirah of Judgement

**Halls of Heaven** Levels of the spiritual realms corresponding to heightened states of awareness and consciousness. There is no single realm of Heaven in Kabbalah but a number of states of spirit.

**Hell**   A low or denser state of consciousness created by the individual themselves.

**Hesed**   Sephirah of Mercy

**Higher Self**   The inner teacher residing at Tiferet (The Seat of Solomon)

**Hod**   Sephirah of Reverberation corresponding to the intellect

**Hokhmah**   Sephirah of Wisdom

**Kabbalah**   To receive – the hidden oral teachings of Jewish mysticism

**Kabbalist**   A practitioner and initiate of Kabbalah

**Keter**   Sephirah of the Crown – highest sephirah on the Tree of Life

**Maaseh Merkabah (Work of the Chariot)**   Archaic name for Kabbalah referring to vehicles of ascent (ritual, devotion and contemplation)

**maggid**   Instructor or teacher

**Malkhut**   Sephirah of the Kingdom – lowest point on the Tree of Life

**mysteries**   The esoteric teachings of the ancients preserved and added to by successive mystics

**Nezah**   Sephirah of Eternity

**pathworking**   A form of guided meditation used to explore the unconscious and the spiritual dimensions

*Sefer ha Yetzirah*   Book of Formation

*Sefer ha Zohar*   Book of Splendour

**sephirah (*pl.* sephiroth)**   Symbolic vessel representing the attributes of God

**Talmud**   The written record of the oral teaching and commentaries on the Bible

**Tarot**   Seventy-eight cards used for divination and psychic readings

**third eye**   Sensory organ in the subtle body factilitating psychic sight / perception

**Tiferet**   Sephirah of Beauty

**Torah (*Sefer ha Torah*)**   Book of Instruction

**Yesod**   Sephirah of Foundation

**Yezirah**   World of Formation – the psychological realm

# Useful Addresses

## Canada

*Kabbalah Centre of Toronto*, 678 Sheppard Avenue West, Toronto, Ontario M3H 2S5, Canada. Tel: (1) 416 631 9395. Website: http://torontokabbalah.com/ or e-mail info@torontokabbalah.com (Provides events and courses (associated with Z'ev ben Shimon Halevi).)

## Israel

*Bnei Baruch Organisation,* PO Box 584, Bnei Brak 51104, Israel. Tel: 972 3 619 1301 or 972 3 618 0731. Fax 972 3 578 1795. Website: http://www.kabbalah-web.org or e-mail bnei-baruch@kabbalah-web.org (An orginisation which disseminates the wisdom of the Kabbalah in accordance with the teachings of Rabbi Y. Ashlag (1882–1955) and his son Rabbi Baruch Ashlag (1906–91). They teach in 3 languages – Hebrew, English and Russian – and offer lectures, courses, seminars, workshop as well as

publishing books and other information.)
*The Holy Yeshiva Kabbalah Academy*, Shaar Hasamaim,
Jerusalem can be reached through their websites:
http://shemayisrael.co.il or
http://194.90.124.37/shaar_hasamaim/academy.htm
(More traditional, orthodox based, combines the teaching of
the Torah with Kabbalah.)

## Switzerland

*Spiritweb Org* can be contacted via their website
 http://www.spiritweb.org/spirit/kabbalah.htm or
e-mail: info@spiritweb.org
(Established in 1993, the organisation promotes spiritual
consciousness on the Internet.)

## UK

*Centre for Kabbalah Studies,* 148 Finchley Lane, London NW4
(Run courses on the Kabbalah, write to the above address for
further information.)
*Warrren Kenton*, Flat 2, 31–3 Priory Road, London, NW6
(Private tutoring in Way of Kabbalah courses.)
*Department of Hebrew and Jewish Studies*, University College
London, Gower Street, London, WC1E 6BT. Tel: 0171 380
7171, Fax: 0171 209 1026.
Website: http://ucl.ac.uk/hebrew-jewish or
e-mail: uclhhjs@ucl.ac.uk
(Undergraduate, postgraduate and MA courses together with
lectures and seminars covering all aspects of Judaism.)

## USA

*Kabbalah Society,* Principal Director, Kabbalah Society, 100 Broadway, PO Box 531, Lynbrook, NY 11563, USA.
Tel: (1) 516 887 4957.
Website: http://www.kabbalahsociety.org or
e-mail: webmaster@kabbalahsociety.org
(Conferences, lectures, workshop and articles.)
*School of Spritual Integrity* based in California, can be reached through their website
http://lady_kythera_ann.fortunecity.com/kabbalah.html or
e-mail: kythera@angelic.com
(The school was founded by Reverend Kythera Ann in 1988 and it offers courses locally or by mail in various metaphysical disciplines, including contemplative and meditative Kabbalah.)
*Kabbalah Centres of Florida* can be contacted through their website:
http://www.kabbalah.com/sitemap.html or
e-mail kabbalah@icanect.net
*Theosophic Kabbalah* is currently being explored on a private website at the University of California, Davis:
http://philo.ucdavis.edu or
e-mail jcpickett@ucdavis.edu

## Other Judaism net links:

http://judaism.miningco.com/msub.kabbalah.htm for information and resources
http://www.metzia.com/ use this Jewish Search Directory for exploring Jewish websites for what you need.

# Further Reading

Andrews, Ted, *Simplified Magic: A Beginner's Guide To The New Age Qabala*, Llewellyn, 1995

Fortune, Dion, *The Mystical Qabalah*, Aquarian Press/ HarperCollins, 1987

Halevi, Z'ev ben Shimon, *Kabbalah: Tradition of Hidden Knowledge*, Thames and Hudson, 1992

Halevi, Z'ev ben Shimon, *Psychology and Kabbalah*, Gateway Books, 1991

Halevi, Z'ev ben Shimon, *The Way of Kabbalah*, Gateway Books, 1991

Halevi, Z'ev ben Shimon, *The Work of the Kabbalist*, Gateway Books, 1993

Kaplan, Aryeh, *Sefer Yetzirah*, Weiser, 1997

Regardie, Israel, *The Golden Dawn*, Llewellyn, 1997

Roland, Paul, *Revelations: The Wisdom of the Ages*, Carlton, UK/Ulysses Press, 1995

Roland, Paul, *Prophecies and Predictions*, S Webb & Son/ Orbis, 1997

Roland, Paul, *The Complete Book of Dreams*, Hamlyn, 1999

Roland, Paul, *Angels: A Piatkus Guide*, Piatkus, 1999

# Index